Lois B. Hart, Ed.D., president of Leadership Dynamics, is a consultant, speaker, and author of books and training materials, including *Moving Up! Women and Leadership*.

J. David Dalke, D. Min., co-director of Learnings Unlimited, is a counselor, consultant, and author.

Both authors have lectured extensively on the subject of work and conflict.

THE SEXES AT WORK

Improving Work Relationships Between Men and Women

LOIS B. HART
J. DAVID DALKE

A SPECTRUM BOOK

Prentice-Hall, Inc., Englewood Cliffs, New Jersey 07632

Library of Congress Cataloging in Publication Data

Hart, Lois Borland.
  The sexes at work.

  "A Spectrum Book."
  Includes index.
  1. Sex role in the work environment.   I. Dalke, J.
  David   II. Title.
  HF5387.H37 1982   306'.36   82-12303
  ISBN 0-13-807321-X
  ISBN 0-13-807313-9 (pbk.)

1 2 3 4 5 6 7 8 9 10

ISBN 0-13-807321-X {PBK.}

ISBN 0-13-807313-9

Editorial/production supervision by Alberta Boddy
Cover design © 1983 by Jeannette Jacobs
Manufacturing buyer: Cathie Lenard

Prentice-Hall International, Inc., *London*
Prentice-Hall of Australia Pty. Limited, *Sydney*
Prentice-Hall of Canada, Ltd., *Toronto*
Prentice-Hall of India Private Limited, *New Delhi*
Prentice-Hall of Japan, Inc., *Tokyo*
Prentice-Hall of Southeast Asia Pte. Ltd., *Singapore*
Whitehall Books Limited, *Wellington, New Zealand*
Editora Prentice-Hall do Brasil Ltda., *Rio de Janeiro*

To Arn and Annie

CONTENTS

PREFACE

You are about to read a book packed with pain and opportunity. It talks about women and men who live side by side, day after day, in the work world. We have written about life in the work force—what it is and what it possibly can be. We write about equality and justice. A truth we discovered is that there are no heroes or heroines in working relationships that are productive and meaningful. There are simply divisions of labor.

Our research has been a combination of sensitizing, learning, and osmosis. Before and during the actual writing of this text, our own conditioned thoughts dramatically changed concerning what a woman *should* be and what a man *ought* to accomplish. It has been an exciting experience reevaluating the traditional work roles.

As you read the following pages, new ideas and concepts may spring upon you when you least expect them. In fact, you may feel as though your mind has been seduced into considering some concepts you never entertained before. We feel that this is symbolic of where men and women are in their quest for understanding each other. Answers come forth without knowing specifically how such an answer or idea emerged.

We also know that what you read here is only a nibble at the subject of survival for men and women working together. This book does not attempt to eliminate the gender prejudices that have been created in the past; rather, it offers an awareness of a new direction. We want our words to seep into the working person. It has happened this way for us and it can happen to you, too. Osmosis is contagious.

Our project has been met with enthusiastic support from both men and women who have encouraged, questioned, and prodded us to put our findings and ideas into print. There is a longing to challenge the inequities at all work levels and in all types of organizations. We hope as you read our book that some thoughts for change will spark inside of you as they have in us. If that happens, we just may be on our way, together, not only to more nearly equal working relationships, but to more nearly equal living relationships as well.

We are grateful for the assistance of the many individuals in our research who gave so willingly of their time, energy, and creativeness. We acknowledge Kathleen McAngus for her help in designing and testing our questionnaire instrument. We appreciate Ann Kauffman, Margaret Rush, Lou Isaacson, and Jimmy Isaacson for evaluating our manuscript and facilitating our research groups. We offer our thanks to Ada Lou Hammons for editing and typing our final manuscript. And last, this book would not have been possible without the many persons who participated in the research groups, who completed our questionnaire, and who participated in the personal interviews.

1

THE "PINCH"

Before I knew my place—
Now all that's changed:
Comfort is behind me;
Adventures are ahead.
But it still hurts.

Times have changed drastically for men and women, in both their personal and work lives. Before, we knew where we belonged; we knew what it meant to be a woman or a man. Roles were clearly defined, and we played them out as we were taught. It was safe and comfortable to stay in a role that was predictable.

But it is different now. No longer are roles clearly defined. We don't have to look far to see examples of how roles, traditionally held by women or men, are changing.

Increasing numbers of women are returning to school to prepare themselves for the world of work. *Time* magazine's latest analysis of career women revealed, "Women represented one-third of last year's freshman class in leading law schools such as Harvard, Yale, Columbia, and Stanford. In addition, about 30 percent of the 1978-79 freshmen classes of leading medical and graduate business schools were women."[1]

[1] "Women as Management Presence," *Management Review*, October 1979, p. 4.

Marshall Loeb, economics editor for *Time*, predicts that "the most important social development in our nation in the 1980s will be the continuing rise to positions of power and influence by American women."[2]

This trend is in full swing: Women are moving outside the traditional four areas in which they have been working—clerical, service, factory, and sales. They are now becoming airline pilots, engineers, doctors, oil drillers, and executives.

Men are shifting roles, too. There is an increase in the number of men teaching young children, heading schools and libraries, and working in nursing and clerical positions. They are also refusing transfers as a part of professional advancement in order to maintain a stable and meaningful family life. Opportunities for advancement to a higher level position in management are not automatically accepted by men. Rather, they are weighing the price with the potential rewards. But it hurts. When we leave the security of the past behind and dare to venture into unknown territory, we experience the exhilaration of new adventure and the pain that comes with change and growth.

Thus, men and women are both feeling the "pinch"—that uncomfortable and uneasy feeling one gets when one's present experience doesn't match one's learning from the past. The pinch is present when we know something is wrong; when we worry, wonder, and search for answers.

WHO'S FEELING THE PINCH?

As professional trainers and counselors we have had the opportunity to interact frequently with men and women working in varied occupations and at various levels in their organizations. We have noticed who is feeling the pinch the most and who is choosing to do something about it.

The loudest cries of pain have come from women. Throughout the 1970s women told the world, "We know there is more to life than how it was defined to us while we were growing up, and we want to be an active part of the working world," but "Oh, how it hurts to have to fight so much for the opportunity to use our skills and education, to be accepted

[2] Ibid.

for what we can contribute at work, to have a personal life and meaningful work, too." The cries came in many forms: from whimpers of pain expressed at home, to formation of women's groups, to protest marches, to class-action suits.

When women began to get in touch with themselves, men were swept along, whether or not they wanted to be. Paul Gallaway, a writer for the *Chicago Sun Times,* sharply points out, "Men, in general, are reacting and adjusting to the unfettered women—very poorly in many instances."[3] At home, they are pinched with demands to share household tasks and to express their emotions more openly. At work, men feel pinched when forced to work for a woman boss.

THE ORGANIZATION
FEELS THE PINCH, TOO

The organization has suffered, also, as these men and women were struggling for a redefinition of their roles. We believe that the following problems faced in today's work places have some relationship to the fact that men and women are not only uncomfortable working with each other, but that solutions have not yet been found.

Employee Attitude. Daily we hear complaints from employers saying that today's employees are difficult to work with. They tell us, "What's wrong is the attitude of today's workers." "I can't motivate them." "Their meaning of work is so different from mine."

Attitudes are based on individual values and beliefs, and they form the basis of one's behavior. Today's employees reflect diverse attitudes, not only because they grew up in different generations and sections of the country, but also because growing up male is a very different experience from growing up female. Therefore, as more and more women entered the work force, different attitudes entered as well.

Many employees, as well as employers, are uncomfortable with having to work with and for people with whom they have never worked before. We hear such comments as, "I'd rather have a male boss." "If

[3]Paul Gallaway, "Listen Guys: Women Have Changed a Lot," *Chicago Sun Times,* January 13, 1980.

only a woman would think more like a man." Men don't understand women's attitudes, and women don't understand men's!

Employee Selection and Retention. Finding and keeping the best possible employees are legitimate goals of employers. However, that pool of candidates has shifted—They are more educated, younger, and more mobile. Adding to this pinch, employers are also increasingly bound by new federal regulations affecting employee selection procedures, beginning with affirmative action extending to actual questions that may or may not be asked in job interviews.

In spite of efforts made to select the best candidate, employee turnover is a major personnel problem. Today's employees stay with one organization less than five years, a costly item for organizations. The costs come out in time and money to search again for the best candidate and to orient and train the new person. For example, an Army study showed that women recruits were failing to finish their first enlistments at a much higher rate than male volunteers. The estimates were that 46.7% of the women would drop out compared with 33.2% of the men. All four reasons listed for this high turnover rate, according to Kathleen Carpenter of the Pentagon, related to problems women faced working with men and vice versa.[4]

Productivity. Today's managers are also upset by the trend toward lower productivity. Since productivity is measured not only in terms of products manufactured but also in terms of services rendered, the problem is found everywhere: in higher education, manufacturing, government, and social agencies. Causes of lowered productivity are traced to people problems. Poorly managed people produce less. Lack of opportunity to make significant contributions and to develop professionally result in employee dissatisfaction.

We are suggesting that men as well as women experience these problems, both as employees and as managers; however, they experience them in different ways. Thus, the way those of each gender group perceive these problems and assist in their remedy will affect future productivity.

---

[4]"Women Army Recruits Dropping Out Early," *Times-Call*, Longmont, Colorado, Oct. 22, 1980.

WHAT CAN YOU DO?

If you are someone who is struggling through this transitional period, and most likely you are since you picked up this book, what can you do to cope with the rapidity and complexity of changes you are facing?

Figure 1-1 will help you understand what happens when we feel the pinch.[5] We start a new job with certain defined expectations of our

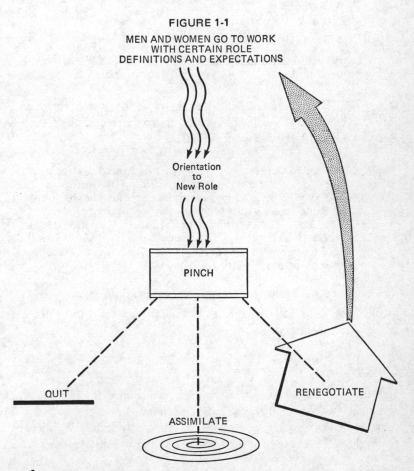

FIGURE 1-1

MEN AND WOMEN GO TO WORK
WITH CERTAIN ROLE
DEFINITIONS AND EXPECTATIONS

Orientation
to
New Role

PINCH

QUIT

ASSIMILATE

RENEGOTIATE

[5]Material on pages 5-8 is adapted from John J. Sherwood and John C. Glidewell, "Planned Renegotiation: A Norm-Setting OD Intervention," in W. W. Burke (Ed.), *Contemporary Organization Development: Conceptual Orientations*

roles and of those around us. Try to remember the last time you started a new job, and recall what you expected of your new boss, your colleagues, and yourself. Did any of those spoken, written, or implied role expectations come from traditional definitions of what were appropriate behaviors for men and women? If they did, you'll recognize them in the following thoughts of Robert, the boss, and his new subordinate, Betty.

> *Robert:* Well, Betty appears to be well educated and also good looking. Our customers will like that. Perhaps I can assign her the project my boss gave to me because I'm not sure I want to do it myself.
>
> *Betty:* I'm so grateful to get this job; I'll work extra hard to keep it. He sure knows all the answers; I'm glad he'll be here to tell me what to do.

Robert and Betty may not even feel the pinch because both sound like they are comfortable with their roles. But let's reverse their positions. Robert is hired by Betty to work for her.

> *Betty:* He seemed uncomfortable when I expressed my feelings about our work and the others in the office. That may be a problem for him; however, he is the most qualified for the job. Will he also question my authority like his predecessor did?
>
> *Robert:* I've never had a woman boss. She is attractive and that is certainly distracting. I hope she doesn't talk about her feelings too much because I don't know what to say. This is surely different from working for Samuel.

What can Robert and Betty do? Like you and others facing a disruption or challenge of established role expectations, there are three choices as shown in the figure.

Choice One—Quit

Quitting is a radical, but understandable, solution if the individual faces continual frustration that produces increased stress and anxiety. For instance, if Robert, the subordinate, is constantly kidded by his friends for working for a lady boss or if he can't accept her style of management,

and Interventions. (Washington, D.C.: NTL Institute for Applied Behavioral Sciences, 1972), pp. 35-46. © Sherwood & Glidewell, 1971.

or if he finds her attractiveness too distracting, he might choose to quit his job.

Or if Betty, the boss, finds it increasingly difficult to supervise Robert because he undermines or ignores her authority and her superiors don't support her, or if she finds she can't communicate with him because their styles are so different, she might choose to look for another job.

One disadvantage of this option is that those who quit—who give up—may be misled into thinking that the problem is solved. More likely what happens is that Robert, or Betty, quickly discovers similar role expectations in a new position. Thus, the "pinch" returns.

A second disadvantage of choosing the option of quitting, beyond the obvious loss caused by employee turnover, is that the underlying issues causing the pinch will never be faced by those left behind—the boss, colleagues, and subordinates. Thus, the pinch reappears when the next person is hired.

Choice Two—Assimilate

Another option to take when the "pinch" occurs is to leave things the way they are. This means accepting the established values, attitudes, behaviors, and roles in the organizations. Al and Alice are two professionals who made the choice to remain in their positions and to assimilate and maintain the status quo.

Al, a manager with a large business, wants a more flexible work schedule so that he can spend more time with his wife, who works an evening shift. His efforts are continually thwarted by upper management. After many requests are turned down, he gives up and decides to maintain the usual office hours of his company. Although he appears to have resolved the problem, Al is still aware of the pull between his spouse and his work, and he carries unspoken resentment toward his employer.

Alice quickly learned she was expected to dress according to the tradition of the banking business. When she tried to adapt the classic uniform to her style and existing wardrobe, she was counseled by her boss and warned by one colleage that she had better conform. After six months of discomfort and soul-searching, Alice assimilated; she purchased a new wardrobe and now looks like everyone else. She denies that this bothers her; however, there are clues that behind her words there is a regret that she gave into a norm that was less compatible with her style.

Holding a status-quo position invites a continual pinch. Very few things change. No one deals with the problem causing the pinch. Thus, the issue goes round and round, never going anywhere, as the symbol for assimilation shows in Figure 1-1.

Choice Three—Renegotiate

Instead of quitting or assimilating into the norms of the majority or of the most powerful, men and women have the choice of renegotiating their roles. This requires admission of the extent of the pinching and of the causes of the hurt. It requires acceptance of one another's pains, hopes, and needs. Both must listen, review, compromise, and then grow in a new direction. Our book is about professional men and women who admit they are being pinched, who are searching for answers, who are willing to renegotiate their roles together, and who recognize the journey must be shared. As authors, we did not get to this point easily either. Here is how we became involved.

HOW WE BEGAN

Not so long ago we did not even notice there was a problem. We, perhaps like you, gradually got an uneasy feeling that something was wrong. We felt personally "pinched" in our lives. We opened our eyes and saw how pervasive "the pinch" was; we felt we could not ignore the problems any longer.

We wanted to take positive steps to help. Two routes emerged. One was to explore the traditions, policies, and procedures of organizational life. At the time we recognized, and still do, that the organizational structure, systems, and norms contribute heavily to these problems. However, we chose a second approach.

We initially focused on those who expressed their pain the loudest— women. We thought we could help them adjust to their new life styles and roles at work. We counseled them. We presented programs for them.

We wrote books for them.[6] But this approach, although well-meaning and appropriate at the time, was inadequate for two reasons. First, meaningful changes at work require the involvement of all who work there, not just the women. Our efforts were less effective when we focused only on the women. This one-sided approach merely tended to encourage assimilation of the women into the male culture.

Second, we were ignoring the other half of the work population—the men. We suspected they were hurting also. Seldom were the men asked what they thought and felt and what they needed and wanted during this transitional period.

We decided to ask.

WHAT AND WHO?

Primarily, we needed to determine *what to ask*. We combed our own work experiences and those of other professionals. We listed the areas in the work place in which we knew women and men were experiencing conflict with each other; we revised and tested until we were ready to gather the information we sought.

We determined twelve categories of potential conflict, and we wondered if men and women were experiencing these problems differently. The following topics and questions were developed into a written questionnaire to use in our interviews.[7]

1. *Etiquette:*	Who opens doors; who pays for meals and drinks? How does one handle shaking hands?
2. *Language:*	What word should be used to describe the female gender—woman or lady—or to describe certain roles—chairman or chairperson?
3. *Emotions:*	How do others perceive one's style of expressing emotions?
4. *Sexual Behavior and Language:*	Does one receive unwarranted sexual remarks and propositions?

[6]Lois B. Hart, *Moving Up! Women and Leadership,* New York: AMACOM, 1980.
[7]Pages 149-168 outline procedures used to validate the content of the questionnaire, explain the two forms used (male and female versions), and include a copy of the cover letter and questionnaires used.

5. *Sexual Attractiveness:* Is one excessively distracted when sexually attracted to someone of the opposite gender at work?

6. *Meetings:* Is it difficult convincing others to accept your ideas, to share power in decision-making, and to receive recognition for one's work?

7. *Authority:* Is one's authority accepted?

8. *Motivation:* Do other people question why one is working?

9. *Expectations:* Are expectations different for one individual than for another of the opposite gender who has a similar role?

10. *Opportunities:* Is it hard to obtain opportunities for advancement?

11. *Separating Work and Home:* How hard is it to separate work responsibilities from demands in one's personal life, such as child care, overtime, travel for the job?

12. *Privileges and Benefits:* How does one resolve the fact that one may be receiving fewer privileges and benefits, and less money than someone of the opposite gender?

Next, we had to decide *who to ask.* We immediately ruled out those who denied there was any problem between women and men at work and those who quit or accepted assimilation as the solution. We wanted to hear from the workers who would admit experiencing the "pinch" and from those who were making attempts to resolve these problems, perhaps through renegotiation of their work roles and relationships.

We decided to interview men and women who were currently in professional roles or in supervisory and management positions, in both profit and nonprofit organizations located in different geographical regions, and who ranged in age from their twenties to near retirement. The majority of the interviews were done through correspondence using the questionnaire. As we continued to probe for explanations and solutions, we personally interviewed many individuals, held small research study groups, and explored the issues in workshop settings.[8]

We asked those we interviewed to focus on particular male-female relationships, not to generalize on their experience with "all other women"

[8] See Appendix II (page 169) for further explanation of criteria used to select samples, how many questionnaires were distributed, who responded, and other sources used to gather information.

or "all other men." Each person was asked to focus on individuals of the opposite gender in these categories: a boss, a subordinate, and a colleague.

Our research had two major purposes: First, did women and men face these conflicts to the same degree?; and second, what was each group doing about it? To find answers to the first question we asked each person twelve questions based on the twelve conflict areas we outlined earlier. Each was asked to rate how serious the problem was for him or her. (See Appendix I for examples and especially to compare how the questions were worded differently in some categories for the two gender groups.)

To fulfill the second purpose, we asked them what problem-solving steps and strategies they were using to resolve the conflicts, if they handled them alone or with others, and how successful they had been. Each person elaborated on any three of the problem areas, preferably those they indicated to be of major importance.

THE RESULTS

We discovered some startling differences in the ways men and women viewed each other. We re-discovered that, in the last decade, we have *not* come a long way after all. We reaffirmed that, although the organization will need to institute lasting changes, it is the person-to-person relationship, the man-to-woman relationship, that will determine success.

Based on our research, we believe that, although differences in age, ethnicity, and race or the balance of power inherent in the boss-employee relationship exacerbate problems, the real culprit is based on differences of gender.

The statistics from our answers to the twelve questions are tabulated in Table 1-1 and illustrate that women perceive these problems more frequently than men do. One-third to two-thirds of the women were experiencing problems in eleven of the categories. The men's frequency of experience ranges from less than 1% to 44%. In only one category did men indicate they experienced the conflicts more often than women— that of sexual attractiveness. The perceived difference is 15%.

Closest in perception—only 1%—is the response to the question about whether or not women receive equal benefits and privileges.

TABLE 1-1 Summary of Part II on the Questionnaire

CATEGORIES	ANSWERED YES BY		DIFFERENCE (IN %) PERCEIVED MORE FREQUENTLY BY	
	Women	Men	Women	Men
Authority	65%	03%	64.7%	
Meetings	66%	17%	49%	
Motivation to Work	35%	07%	34.3%	
Expression of Emotions	53%	26%	27%	
Etiquette	35%	13%	22%	
Language	53%	32%	21%	
Expectations	41%	25%	16%	
Opportunities	42%	25%	17%	
Sexual Behavior and Language	44%	28%	16%	
Separating Work and Home	42%	26%	16%	
Sexual Attractiveness	17%	32%		15%
Benefits and Privileges	43%	44%		1%

Next we sought to identify exactly how serious each problem is to men and women alike. They were asked to rate each of the twelve problems on a scale of one to five (one representing a minor problem and five a major conflict). As researchers, we decided to consider the conflicts given ratings of either four or five as major problems. The statistics, as listed in Table 1-2, reveal that neither men nor women were experiencing these problems as seriously as perhaps is initially suggested in Table 1-1. For instance, authority is mentioned earlier as a problem by 65% of the women, but only 43% perceive it as serious.

The data illustrate that men found most of these problems relatively minor since areas rated as major conflicts were circled by only 0% to 21% of them. Also the range of differences between men and women, which ran from 1% to 28.4%, is considerably smaller than indicated in Table 1-1.

The preliminary information as shown in these two tables validated our own perceptions at the time that men and women were *both* struggling with a variety of problems during what could be considered a transi-

TABLE 1-2 Summary of Part III on the Questionnaire

CATEGORIES	RATED A MAJOR PROBLEM BY		DIFFERENCES
	Women	Men	
Authority	43%	12%	31%
Meetings	29%	06%	28.4%
Motivation to Work	16%	02%	15.8%
Expression of Emotions	23%	13%	10%
Etiquette	3%	0%	3%
Language	22%	03%	21.7%
Expectations	—	—	—
Opportunities	33%	15%	18%
Sexual Behavior and Language	28%	12%	16%
Separating Work and Home	19%	13%	6%
Sexual Attractiveness	18%	17%	1%
Benefits and Privileges	36%	21%	15%

tional period of role changing. The data merely gave us a launching point from which we could explore deeper into the causes and solutions to these conflicts.

The goal of *The Sexes at Work* is to present a balanced description of the work conflicts that both men and women are experiencing, along with a description of what successes they are having in resolving these conflicts.

LOOKING DEEPER

The next twelve chapters explore deeply each of the conflicts experienced by men and women. We attempt to interpret the statistics, present real cases of professional men and women, and suggest solutions and recommendations. Although we reach some conclusions, we also raise new questions.

Before you begin to read the book, we suggest you become more familiar with (and even complete) the questionnaire in Appendix I. We suggest you read slowly and think about what you are reading. Apply the ideas that would work best in your own situation. Pick and choose carefully. This book has been written so that you can read the chapters in any order you wish, choosing those areas of discussion that have caused you the most problems.

Do not get discouraged or overwhelmed as you read. Try not to yield to the natural tendency to make changes in all the areas at once. This is not possible, nor is it helpful. Work at the changes one by one. Remember, a little is better than nothing.

Try to get others involved by reading the book or a few chapters simultaneously. Discuss the ideas and solutions, and together compare notes and adopt changes that would improve your relationships. This last suggestion is crucial, since the goal of our research is to get men and women to communicate with each other, to face these conflicts together, and to explore solutions together. Therefore, reading, discussing, and planning together will ensure a higher level of success in reaching across differences caused by differences in gender.

Who will benefit? *You* will. Men and women, out of necessity, must work together toward the achievement of their personal and organizational goals. Reaching across our differences *is* possible. Let's see how it can be done.

WHY DO YOU WORK?

Have you ever been asked, "Why *do* you work?" or perhaps asked in another way, "Why do *you* work?" The word emphasized makes a difference in how you would answer the question. The first version most likely explores your motive for working and is a legitimate question asked by career counselors, who try to help you clarify the meaning of work in your life. The second version questions why *you*, a particular individual, work—a less legitimate question because it may be perceived as a challenge.

As professionals who have worked with men and women in many kinds of occupations, we have heard both questions asked. We have observed that women are asked why *they* work more frequently than their male colleagues, spouses, and brothers. For this reason we have included this potential area of conflict between men and women in our survey and investigation.

Initially, we asked the women, "Have you ever been questioned why you work?" Thirty-five percent said yes, although, when ranked relative to the other twelve categories of conflict, only 16% felt it was a major problem.

The men were asked if they had ever questioned why women work, and the response was low—only .07% admitted they had. This is not too surprising since our male respondents were also trying hard to adjust to the new world of working with women.

At first glance it would appear that a person's motivation for working is not a serious problem, at least not as serious as it was a decade ago. However, when we looked below the surface answers, we discovered three shifts, or changes, that have occurred over the past ten years: Women are questioned less; men question the role of work more; and motives for work are different. In this chapter we address the question of how one measures motivation and who does the measuring. We cover six situations in which the question, "Why do you work?" is most likely to be asked.

THREE SHIFTS

We found the issues surrounding work motivation shifting in three ways.

Women Are Questioned Less.   The professional women we surveyed appear to be asked the question less frequently than they were even ten years ago. We think that over the past decade, it has been increasingly accepted that women work for the same primary reason that men do—to earn money. As the income figures below indicate, double-digit inflation has forced more and more married women into the workplace because two incomes are needed to maintain their standard of living.[1]

Income of Working Women's Husbands

10%	Under $7,000
8%	$7,000-$9,999
15%	$10,000-$14,999
23%	Over $15,000
56%	

The remaining working women (44%) are usually not questioned why they work; 25% of these fall into the "never married" category and 19% are widowed, divorced, or separated.

The 1980 Virginia Slims American Women's Opinion Poll reaffirms what the U.S. Department of Labor states. Of women now employed

[1]Women's Bureau, Office of the Secretary, Bureau of Labor Statistics, U.S. Department of Labor, Aug. 1979.

43% said they worked to supplement the family income; 27% work to support themselves, and 19% work to support their families. Only 14% said they were working simply because they wanted "something interesting to do."[2]

Men Do More Questioning. Although it is common for men going through their middle-aged years to question the meaning of work and life, we are hearing younger men also question the role of work in their lives. Gail Sheehy found in recent research that men between 18 and 28 whom she interviewed didn't want to work hard; they wanted time for personal growth and desired a perfectly balanced life of work, love, family life, and leisure.[3]

How did this trend in men's changing attitudes start? Was it the changing role of how women's or men's work fits into the purpose of their lives? Probably the former, however, *how* the change began isn't really important; more important is the fact that both men and women *are* asking questions that may enhance the meaning of their work lives. It certainly is a boon to working women that the men with whom they live and work are asking the same questions, because it takes the spotlight off of women as a gender group and on to the activity in which we spend the greatest amount of time—work.

Women's Motives for Working Are Changing. Women's motivation to work appears to be shifting from "I'm doing this for others (my child, my spouse, my parents)," to "I'm working because I have to and I want to." Perhaps this shift is merely indicative of the past decade's tendencies towards "me-centeredness," or perhaps the shift is a natural phase in a human potential movement. Whatever the cause, it exists.

HOW IS MOTIVATION MEASURED?

An underlying question with which we were frequently confronted was,

[2]1980 Virginia Slims American Women's Opinion Poll, Fifth Ave., 100 Park Ave., N.Y. 10017.

[3]Gail Sheehy, "The Truth about Today's Young Men," *Esquire*, October 1979, pp. 25-26.

"How can you measure a person's motivation?" Traditional criteria for measurement are reflected in checklists such as one prepared by a corporate "headhunter," who writes that when searching for key executives, look for items such as work-oriented extracurricular interests, no concern at all for the number of hours worked, and a record of having taken second jobs.[4] If this absolute devotion to work—day and night—measures his (and, we suppose, her) work motivation, then no wonder so many people with whom we talked are in conflict with their employers!

A recent Harris poll studying the effect of work on families revealed a surprising finding: Most women said they would choose part-time employment if they could afford to do so and even if economics weren't a factor. This was even true of women who currently hold executive, managerial, or professional jobs.[5]

But what happens when a woman, or a man for that matter, chooses or must work only part-time due to family responsibilities or health restraints? Deirdre, one woman we interviewed, related to us, "I had worked three years in my professional position when my husband and I decided we should start our family before we were much older. After a six-month leave of absence, I returned to work for three days a week. The issue of conflict appeared to be one of perception—on the part of my boss and my colleagues. At first their shift in attitude toward me was subtle, but eventually I found the root of the problem to be that they no longer perceived me as being dedicated, hardworking, or job-oriented—all because I was not working full-time. My child was seen as taking my loyalty away from the job and focusing it on my family. This perception was partly true. I was responsible for my new baby and my devotion to my work was not total anymore, but I gave the work my full attention while I was there. But the problem remained that my motivation was questioned because I only worked part-time. My male, unmarried colleague was seen as more motivated and valuable to our agency."

<hr/>

[4] "Spotting Job Candidates with a Strong Work Ethic," *Boardroom Reports,* December 29, 1980. Excerpted from John Wareham, *Secrets of a Corporate Headhunter,* Atheneum Publishers.

[5] Judy Klemsdrud, "Working Women Not in It Just for Money," *Times-Call,* May 7, 1981.

WHO MEASURES MOTIVATION?

Who determines what constitutes an appropriate demonstration of motivation or what role work should take in one's life? Reflecting upon society over the past fifty years, we know there was a subtle pressure placed on women in the post-World War II era to return to the home and leave paid work to the men. More recently, men and women who are considering reducing their working hours are often asked, "Don't you think that your skills and education will be wasted if you don't work full-time?" or "But what about your family?"

Some professionals are told outright what they should or should not be doing. Negative comments even come from neighbors and, of course, from well-meaning relatives and employers.

WHEN IS MOTIVATION QUESTIONED?

We found that the question, "Why do you work?" is asked of or at least considered by an individual generally at six particular times: When one is growing up and preparing for one's working life; when one's spouse is earning enough to support the family unit; when a woman's job is seen as taking the place of a job "a man should hold;" when things get "tough on the job;" when a couple is weighing whether or not to have a baby; and when one is selecting a mate. Let us look at each of these separately.

Growing Up. Ask some children, especially teenagers, what they want to do when they grow up, and note what they answer. We found that both boys and girls name many occupations, although girls still name the traditional ones. The girls usually listed wife-mother along with other vocations; the boys did not list father-husband. The girls also indicated, by their words, that they were looking for a *job,* whereas the boys talked about their future *career.* The differences are not only in semantics, but also in one's perspective. A job is something you do, perhaps a time filler or bill payer, but a career is a commitment and thus is serious. All of this deeply affects young people's preparation and motivation for work as adults.

A large number of women who are over thirty-five were given the message as they grew up that work was an option: They could work and then quit to raise a family, go to school, or do good works in the community. (Of course, large numbers of this same group never had these options due to economic reasons.) But when the male colleagues, brothers, and spouses of these same women were asked, "Did you ever think you might have a period in your adult life when you might not work?" they would look at us in shock and respond, "Of course not. I knew I would always work." The women who received these mixed messages and those men who heard it and who later saw women acting it out may be the ones who are now wondering more often why certain women work.

When One Income Suffices. Carrying this problem to the next state of adult life, women may face the question, "Why do you work?" when their husbands earn enough money to support the family. As shown earlier, this may become an even smaller percentage because few families can make ends meet even on $15,000.

Josephine related to us the time when she was upset about not receiving an increase in her salary. Her colleague's response to her complaint was, "What's the problem? Your husband makes good money."

Another professional, Gayle, said her co-worker asked, with obvious envy in his voice, "Why don't you work less hard since your husband is doing so well in his business?"

It works the other way around, too! Bertrand, husband of the successful writer, Letty Pogrebin, related how his colleague (another attorney) sincerely asked, "How come you are still practicing law? I thought you would have retired on your wife's money."[6] Or take the rare case of Ray, a forty-two-year-old executive who decided to quit the rat race of his corporate job and begin the novel he had been wanting to write as well as teach a class at a local college. Financially this was possible because his wife "made enough money." Economic facts aside, the remarks both the husband and wife heard and were told about revealed others' appalled reactions to this arrangement. The comments included, "A 'real man' is the major breadwinner," and "How can you stand living with a woman who makes more money than you do?"

Men Are Threatened. A third time when women may be questioned concerning their motives for working is when men are threatened

---

[6]Letty Pogrebin, *Getting Yours* (New York: David McKay Co., 1975), p. 290.

by the competition women are creating in certain jobs. We recognize that psychologically human beings suppress most feelings and fears. If men openly expressed the real reasons why they are threatened by women's presence at work, the list might include fear of losing status, a job, or a promotion; fear that others might view them as weak or inadequate; and fear of competition with people who had previously not been in the race. To combat the fear, men protect themselves by attempting to reduce the competition. This they do by questioning women's motivation for working, their qualifications, and the practicality of their decisions. The end result is that men manipulate women into thinking it is the women's problem rather than the men's problem of facing their own fears.

Because of the depth of these feelings, most men are not in touch with their fears; therefore, tremendous effort is required to uncover them. In the meantime, comments and questions men raise will continue to be subtle, reflecting their confusion and need to survive.

Work Gets Tough. The fourth instance when one's motivation is challenged is when it gets really tough on the job. We have noted that men generally follow the adage: When the going gets tough, the tough get going. They grit their teeth, accept the rough times, and go on. Men do this, no doubt, because since childhood they never considered they might have the option of not working.

But what are professional women doing? Dee, a banker, told us, "I'm in a no-man's land. I fight so hard to be taken seriously. Just when one barrier is overcome, others seem to emerge. I work so hard and never get the feedback necessary to help me succeed. The result? I'm tired of this nonsense. I don't know how to break through the subtle barriers. Women colleagues and I keep asking why we put ourselves through this hell."

Like the men, many of these women plod along solving one problem after another. But many, like this banker, are considering another option, or is it an "out"? Dee recently had two boys visit in her home. Unlike during her previous contacts with children, this time she literally fell in love with them. Was it because of these particular children? Probably not. Instead it was most likely due to the adverse circumstances at work. When work begins to lose its glory and when the obstacles seem endless, it appears to us that many of these women are considering or even re-considering mothering as a more satisfactory option than work—at least full-time work.

It is commonly said that women work twice as hard for half the credit. An interview with the talented and successful Clare Boothe Luce revealed that when she became a new member of Congress, an "idiotic poll" named her as having "the second best pair of legs in the country, second only to Marlene Dietrich." Following her maiden speech in Congress, which she prepared carefully and delivered eloquently, a male colleague came forward and said, "What they say about you is true—you've got the best-looking pair of legs that have ever been in Congress." Unfortunately this treatment and her extra effort were typical of her long career and caused her to comment, "Had I been a man, I would have received more credit."[7]

Other less-known but equally hard-working women may not ignore these obstacles as readily. They may, instead, find their work commitment lessening. A mental health counselor, Tami, doesn't keep wondering *why* she works, but why she works so *hard* when she only gets minimal recognition. "When I keep 'bankers' hours' or have other 'laid back' behaviors I find I do not respect myself, others question my motives and, of course, the original problems aren't diminished." In Tami's case, she didn't give into the pressure to continue long hours. Instead she "gave herself permission" to be away from her practice more often and made a conscious effort not to respond immediately to every task or project that emerged. She reports a high degree of success, even though she misses out on her share of recognition.

Another way to handle the problem is, rather than reducing one's hours, simply not to work as hard during the working hours. A personnel director who experienced bucking all kinds of direct and subtle attacks and who was especially not being taken seriously says, "I became demotivated. I simply do not have the enthusiasm I initially had. No one says my work is affected, but I know I'm not working as hard. How can I when my heart isn't in it?"

Let's Raise a Family. Couples often ask the big question on work motivation when they are considering having their first child or adding to their family. It's a difficult decision to make—one that many career-oriented couples often ponder for several years. The confusion over the role of work in a woman's life is revealed in Sandra's story. She works in a

[7]*Rocky Mountain News*, Denver, Colorado, December 15, 1980.

community agency for a boss who makes it very clear that he believes women with children should not work. She suspects that if she became pregnant he would insist upon her resignation. Coupled with the other pressures he puts on her, the subtle forms of harrassment, and the lack of support, Sandra says she keeps postponing the decision to have children, so that by now, "I've suppressed my desire to have children, perhaps forever."

Marge and Jim, two professionals, told us that when they had their first child Jim was in school and it was considered all right that he didn't work full time. However Marge found she enjoyed the power that came with being the primary breadwinner. Upon the arrival of their second child they faced a dilemma. How could they continue to meet her professional needs and also provide adequate parenting? From the beginning of their marriage, they recognized that their needs and life styles would change several times. Therefore they were committed to flowing with life's challenges. After evaluation of all options, Marge is currently in a job-sharing position and Jim is working full time, for now anyway.

Selecting a Mate. We found increasing numbers of professionals are more selective in choosing a future mate. One important discussion they engage in together is about the role of work in each of their lives. A young minister, Doug, finds that many of the women he dates admit that they would like to marry and "be taken care of." This is not in Doug's plans. He wants to share the financial burden of a family. He is also worried about what will happen if he should meet a woman whose aspirations are as ambitious as his own and whose motivation to work is as strong as his. Can they meet both needs?

Other couples are finding solutions to this dilemma based on a commitment to their relationship. A director of a conference center where workshops are held in the late spring through early fall solved the problem. Both he and his wife reside at the center during the peak season, and then they live at the place of her college position for the rest of the year. Another couple, both having business concerns, take turns. On an approximate five-year plan, first one partner makes the choice of the next move; then after about five years the other makes the choice. Sure, some promotions may be missed, but they are willing to compromise with each other so that they can be together.

Most of the successes we observed in resolving the demands of two careers occurred when the selection of the future mate was made carefully.

However, we also know of couples who successfully struggled with these issues long after the marriage was established. Generally, though, it was the woman who initiated, pushed, and educated her husband.

WORK IS IMPORTANT, BUT . . .

The role of work is essential to human existence. However, we conclude that the definition of work and the measurement of one's motivation must be made by the individual, regardless of the norms of the organization or of society. If each person were to allow time to reflect on the key question, "Why am I working?" and were then to review the question periodically, more likely employees everywhere would be placed in positions where they could contribute more, where their productivity level would be higher, and where they would be happier as individuals in their work as well as in their personal lives.

The professionals we have contacted believe in one's right to make these decisions; they do not believe in buckling under pressure from others of different opinions. They continually seek a balance between meeting their own needs with those of their family. Communication and compromise exist in their primary relationships. The couples' beliefs and values provide the foundation from which they, as individuals, seek work, negotiate different working conditions, and solve other daily problems that affect their motivation to work. And when, for instance, the employer's policies, procedures, or norms do not mesh with theirs, they present and often fight for change that would meet their personal needs. The battles are never easy, but they are worth the effort because work is an important element in our lives.

3

OF COURSE
I TREAT YOU THE SAME!

"Are you kidding? You want to hire a male to oversee my job? Joe didn't have an overseer. James doesn't have one. Why me? Is it because I am a woman?"

Do these questions indicate a lack of clarity regarding job expectations for Susie, a woman supervisor? We believe they do and that there is a substantial difference in the establishment of job expectations for men versus women. Thus, we purposely designed our research instrument to reflect this. When the women were asked, "Have you ever had a problem accepting or resolving a different set of expectations for your job than what a man might be given," 41% said yes. We asked the men, "Have you ever established a different set of expectations for her (boss, peer, subordinate) job than what you might establish for a man?" To our surprise 25% of the men said yes.

Susie's query, "Is it because I am a woman?" is also the answer and it deserves elaboration. This chapter is designed to point out the discrepancies and discrimination women experience in their work settings. The following four questions we address to women, but they are also intended to help men evaluate their contributions to the problem. This is why the questions carry an impact in our search for solutions and answers.

1. Are your job expectations well defined? Do you know your parameters?
2. Do you experience discrimination in what is expected from male employees and what is expected from female employees?
3. Are the expectations in your present position designed for the position or for you? In other words, would the expectations of the job be the same if a male were hired for your position?
4. Do you feel trusted in your job, and does it have anything to do with being a woman?

Answers to these questions have far-reaching historical roots. What a man or woman carries into a job is not only her or his talents, but an image of who and what society believes him or her to be. The expectations are often stereotypically preconceived ideas of what a man's abilities and roles are as opposed to a woman's abilities and roles.

IMPACT 1: Are Your Job Expectations Well Defined? Or Do You Know Your Parameters?

Kim has been in her present management position for four months. She told us it was a hassle being awarded the job. Some employees felt she prostituted herself sexually with her boss and that had to be the real reason she received the new position with the company. To complicate the transition from a supervisory position to middle management, the expectations were not well defined. She told us, "I did extensive training, but not specifically directed to my job. I was bounced around from one department to another, not being able to establish rapport with the new employees. Even my peers did not communicate well with me. I believe some males would have been more confrontive if they had received the same treatment I did. I felt like I needed to fight for my professional life if I wanted to have this new position. I was babied into setting the limitations of my job. I had several very emotional conversations with my boss. Nothing definitive emerged from our talks. Because my training was so poor no one knew what my expectations were. Even worse, I couldn't get a strong commitment from my boss. I worked in this new office four months; prior to that I had three months training. I am still not sure what parameters I am operating out of from day to day. I may be overly sensitive, but I think a large part of the problem is that I am a woman. Somehow a man seems to command more respect."

Kim feels the lack of definition of her job description puts her in a losing position. She continues, "I'm expected to do everything, whatever that means. It is just not clear where I fit in the system. The chain of command is useless. Now I just write memos to my boss asking for clarification of my role and what is expected of me in relation to my subordinates."

Kim expressed concern and fear that her femaleness hindered her receiving specific definition about her job expectations. She felt like her male superiors were more vague with her than they would have been with a male. Trying not to point fingers she says, "I may be imagining things, but my spasmodic training and the lack of clarity as to my responsibilities seem poorly defined. It's almost like I am programmed to fail."

In further conversations with Kim and Maxine, another working woman, the following suggestions were offered.

Kim: Before taking a work position, particularly in a male-dominated organization, spend hours of personal time with yourself. Bolster your own ego strengths. Define your limits. Know what you want. Be clear how you can integrate meaningfully into the position.

Maxine: I believe you need to check clearly how your own personal assessment of the job limitations fits with the company's expectations. It is essential that you not only understand what is wanted from you, but also that you are able to buy into the limitations.

Kim: I found it very difficult, intellectually and emotionally, to assume a position previously held by a male. Don't forget to be who you are. A woman can't be like any other woman, and for sure not like a man. We, as women, must take our own talents and abilities and fit them into the job expectations and produce in our unique way. It all goes back to what I said earlier: Work hard at knowing what they want and who you are.

Maxine: It is easy to operate out of assumptions. It is also dangerous. Limitations and expectations need definition at the very beginning of the job negotiation.

IMPACT 2: Do You Experience Discrimination in What Is Expected from Male Employees and What Is Expected from Female Employees?

Historically men and women have been viewed not only as physically different, but also as having specifically defined talents, often translated into roles. Since women have long been categorized as homemakers, their credibility in the work world outside the home is limited and often mistrusted. We do not believe most women wish to be treated differently than their male colleagues at work. If a man and woman have the training and talents for making key decisions in the company, both should be given the opportunity. Work positions at all levels of employment should be open to the persons most qualified or potentially believed to be.

Historical roles do cause discrimination at work. A person is often treated differently due to gender rather than ability. Note the emotional flavor of the words from two men commenting about their perceptions of female co-workers. "She is really sloppy and careless. Being her superior I felt it my responsibility to speak to her about such work. I spoke nicely and directly, but I won't do it again. She took it so personally. Now she is moody and miserable to be around." The second statement has the same ring to it: "In evaluating her performance I am more indirect and gentle. However, I am much more harsh and direct with the males on my staff."

The statements reveal a differential attitude of the men who spoke them. A male treats a male one way and a woman another way when the issues at stake are the same. Alice told us her manager gave her the responsibility of following certain policies that she later found did not apply to *all* persons at the plant. Later she observed her boss usurping some of her duties that were described in her job description, without telling her. Her comment was: "Would he [boss] do that to me if I were male? Am I discriminated against and not trusted because I am a woman? Why should the expectations be different because I am female?"

In another case Rebecca revealed she was expected to do *everything* at the office. Men in similar positions were expected to do the same, but they would "pass the buck." She felt her boss condoned the male behavior, but treated her like a servant.

Kim experienced discrimination differently. She felt her boss and her male peers wanted her to be the way they wanted her to be instead of how she really was. "My colleagues say to me, 'Don't be so thin skinned.' I don't think they can handle my honesty, which sometimes comes out in anger. The men I work with swear and say, 'I'll get even!' My outlet feels limited and very controlled. It's lonely."

Such attitudes and expressions of exasperation help identify the problem of discrimination in expectations. All offices and companies do not fall into such an array of dissatisfaction. We are concerned about the ones that overtly or subtly show differential treatment, and we offer accolades to those who operate with a sense of justice and sensitivity.

IMPACT 3: Are the Expectations in Your Present Position Designed for the Position or for You?

Marie, who works for a large corporation with several levels of management, said this to the question cited above. "I know I am competent. I feel I can handle any position in this corporation. Every level here has a job expectation. Some of them are well defined; others are just 'feel your way along.' My present position definitely has expectations. The problem is that it revolves around the person who had this job before me, and he was male. The newspaper business has deadlines. Sometimes they are hard to make. But I have never failed in any assignment on this job. However, I still do not have the respect of my peers who are also in upper management positions. They are all men, too. They are used to the way Scott did this job. They believe I am not doing the work simply because I am not doing it in the way he did it. Also, because I am a female, they (upper management) go around me.

"When I was working my way up to this position, I supervised forty to fifty people in my middle management job. I helped create that place for myself. It worked. I communicated well with the group and had their respect. But I didn't have to follow anyone, especially a male. I think that has hindered me, and some respect for my abilities has been lost. I am good at what I do, but I followed a male and my peers can't seem to allow me the freedom to do the job as I see fit. They expect me to do what Scott did. *I am not Scott!*"

Marie is caught in the grip described by the well-known phrase, "We've always done it this way." She compounds the expectations by being a woman among seven other men, all of equal status, who are key decision-makers in the corporation. Can you imagine an upper-level management meeting in which there were initially seven males and to which one female is then added who has just stepped into a position previously held by a male!

Marie concluded, with a mixture of confidence and anxiety, saying, "I do my job very well. I am competent. I know what needs to be done in this position. The expectations are achieveable. But, I must do things the way I do them. Scott responded to the job his way. I will accomplish the tasks my way. The job is here for anyone who wants to tackle the work. In this case it happens to be me. I don't want any of my subordinates to go around me to my boss. I believe I know what has to be accomplished. Scott and I may work differently, but the job will still get done. The expectations are in line with my abilities. I know gaining the confidence of my employer will take time, but I can do this job."

The issue here lies in allowing Marie to work in her style. The question is that if a man held Marie's position, would he be allowed the freedom to handle the job as he interprets it, according to the job expectations? Employers must keep these issues clearly before them as they monitor whether they treat all employees consistently.

IMPACT 4:   Do You Feel Trusted in Your Job, and Does It Have Anything to Do with Being a Woman?

Trust is a loaded word. Being a working woman in a male-dominated work society is like being on trial. If we put them together—womanhood and trust—we find a situation that is next to impossible to solve. We may come to terms with some individual situations between a man and a woman, but we still live in a society that does not support and affirm equality. The man who instinctively believes in the equality of women finds himself in a lonely position. Trusting a working woman, especially one in authority, would be easier if he were isolated from the pressures of society's traditions and stereotyped roles.

Women tell us they experience little trust in the work world, regardless of whether they are the boss, a peer, or a subordinate. When Katherine was hired as an administrative assistant in a social service agency, she tried everything to build a sense of trust with all levels of employees. To remove traces of her predecessor, she completely rearranged the furniture in her office, which was his old office. She asked to be called by her first name and made herself available at all hours to any of the staff. Her goal was to be accepted and trusted first as a woman and then as an administrative assistant. She knew the agency was testing her. The board of directors, as well as the agency, had high expectations of her. Management positions in the past had been held only by men. Katherine's first year was a time full of elation and wonderment. Gaining a trusting relationship with staff, client, and the community required much energy. At times she felt like giving up and admitting it was a losing battle. When she presented innovative approaches to working with persons and increasing production, her ideas were often heavily scrutinized. Once she asked her male boss, the agency director, to present one of her suggestions to the board and staff. She asked him not to mention the fact that she had spawned the idea. The suggestion was met with enthusiasm and acceptance. Katherine felt like a beggar looking for a handout labeled trust.

In one-to-one situations Katherine received good feedback about her work. In group settings she saw the dynamic of trust change. Interestingly, she noted a lack of support from women colleagues as well as from men. During that first year of her promotion, Katherine began using the age-old female ploy of making her peers and subordinates think her ideas were theirs. She learned to survive, but bitterly.

We asked Katherine if the element of trust was hindered because she was a woman. She said, "There were very few ways I gained the confidence of the staff. I believe if a man had been hired as the administrative assistant, there would have been few trust problems, assuming he was competent. I am capable, too, but it just doesn't seem to matter. I defined the job expectations as clearly as I knew how. Trust was and is very hard to gain. I believe it is because I am a woman."

THE FINAL HOPE

Our research clearly shows that women experience a different set of expectations because of their gender. What can a woman do to close the gap and clarify job expectations? What can men do?

What Can Women Do?

1. Like any employee new to a position, women must clarify both written and unwritten expectations. Read the job description and manual, and then ask questions about how to implement the rules.

Rules may be either formal (written) or informal (assumed).

2. Accept the reality that men and other women may be skeptical of your abilities. Seek outlets for your feelings of isolation by interacting with other women employees who share much the same experience. Deal with the anger and resentment of unfair treatment in a supportive setting. It may not always be appropriate to call the male power structure into question; instead devise, in a supportive fashion, meaningful ways to survive. At any rate, do not deny your feelings.

3. Be assertive when you feel the job expectations are different for women than for men. Prepare your case; speak definitively and with courage.

4. Believe enough in your perceptions to repeat them often. They may be discounted at the onset and several times thereafter, but you have a right to express your observations.

What Can Men Do?

1. If you are a male boss, you can provide explicit written and unwritten expectations to all employees. Many employers provide written job standards. These are an excellent way to avoid discrimination. During the preparation of these materials ask yourself: "Is this job expectation the same as I would determine for a man?"

2. At the beginning, sit down with each new employee and explain the job expectations, seeking to clarify the rules. Also invite her expectations of you and the organization.

3. At the regularly scheduled performance review or at informal feedback sessions, ask the question, "Am I evaluating her performance with the same criteria I would use with a man?" Utilizing the original written and unwritten expectations assures her of a fair review and a place for negotiation if necessary.

4. Males, whether boss, peer, or subordinate, can scrutinize other men's behavior. Bringing to another's awareness his different set of expectations can be an educational attempt for better working relationships. A boss, peer, or subordinate who knows the rules and who can agree to them helps lay the foundations for maintaining and possibly increasing job production. Being definitive in work expectations can only add positive results.

WADE INTO THE TASK

We believe that any time people reach across differences, this implies the desire to to something active (reach across) and the implication that we are all unique (differences). Actively recognizing our individualities as females and males can lower the threat of rigid expectations. Another way to say this is: I, as a worker, am asked to give as much of myself as I am able, to as much of the job as I understand. This requires knowledge of and agreement to operate within the given expectations.

It is important to keep the expectations clear. We feel most jobs can be performed by either a male or female as long as the job analysis is definitive and the training offered is of high quality.

James Thurber's short story, *The Scotty Who Knew Too Much,* tells the tale of a Scotty dog who went to the country to fight two particular animals that frightened the farm dogs. One animal had a white stripe down its back; the other had quills. As the Scotty waded in to eliminate or hurt his opponent, the farm dogs kept saying, "Don't you want to ask any questions, Scotty?"

"No, these are just simple, scrawny animals who don't know how we city dogs fights," replied the Scotty.

After nearly being destroyed in two different encounters with the "simple" animals, the Scotty was so distressed he decided to fight the farm dogs. He put one paw over his nose to ward off the awful vitriol smell; the other paw to shield his eyes from the daggers. Scotty was so badly beaten that the farm dogs sent him to a care home in the city.

Thurber's moral: It's better to ask some of the questions than to know all the answers.

Our moral: Clarify the expectations; ask the questions; then wade into the task.

4

WHO'S
IN CHARGE HERE?

The word *authority* conjures up many responses. It is a word that means power, dictatorship, manipulation, and security. It can be received with respect or bantered about with hostility. Authority, and the use or misuse of it, is a key concept in the world of people and more particularly in the world of work.

It is not surprising, then, that our research points out the largest discrepancy between women and men in the work world occurs in the area of authority. Sixty-five percent of the women surveyed saw authority as a problem, whereas only 0.03% of the men perceived it as problematic. The astounding gap of recognition raises the following questions:

- Is our society still operating out of the concept:

$$\frac{\text{King} \;\; = \;\; \text{Men}}{\text{Servant} \;\; = \;\; \text{Women}}$$

- Is the world of work still the one last hope for men to exaggerate their power?

- Is authority on the job the most difficult for women to break through in regards to equal rights?
- Is the low mention of authority in our survey an indicator that men are afraid to recognize the authority question as a problem?
- Is yielding power at work attacking a man's sense of competitiveness, and thus his control?
- Do men believe women to be inferior in business and incapable of handling authority?
- Do women unwittingly give men the power?
- Is there any hope that women will impact the working world in a significant way?

Another revealing fact from our research centers on the importance of the authority question. Of the women who saw it as a problem, 43% of them identified authority as the major problem of all areas surveyed. For the men, only 12% who saw it as a problem said it was the major concern. It may seem hopeful that one-tenth of the male population surveyed believe the authority issue needs to be addressed. It may also be that men are resenting a woman's need for power and thus feel usurped. This is not as hopeful. Are men and women wanting something quite different to happen in the chain of command, or are those 12% males saying "stay off my back!"?

Here are some of the dynamics we discovered in our research. These situations are compilations of several examples sent to us, but are representative of both genders and explore problems faced with bosses, peers, and subordinates.

Case 1:   The Overcompensating Female Boss

• *Problem area:*   Linda overcompensates in an effort to prove her authority, as viewed by Bob.

• *Type of work relationship:*   Linda is Bob's boss.

• *Work setting:*   Hospital.

• *Example of problem:*   Linda's skills as the head of the X-ray department are not questioned. She is very competent. Bob is new in the department and is eager to learn, but he feels overpowered by Linda's incessant need to prove herself. She continually criticizes Bob's efforts and belittles his apparent lack of knowledge. When he makes mistakes, she takes that opportunity to remind him of his inadequacies and makes cutting comments like, "I thought men were always capable at technical things."

• *Efforts made to resolve the problem:* Bob feels the situation is more than a question of his competency. He believes it is an opportunity for Linda to exercise her power as a woman, thus making it a female-male struggle. He feels undertones of resentment concerning his maleness. Bob seeks out another woman in the department for advice. He feels reticent to confront Linda for fear the opportunity will give her more reason to exercise her strength and tackle his weakness. So far, he is choosing to live with the situation in hopes of moving out of the department. The degree of success seems minimal.

Case 2: Assuming Extra Authority

• *Problem area:* Paul, twenty-two years younger than Barbara, thinks she assumes more authority than is granted by her position.

• *Type of work relationship:* Barbara and Paul are peers, although Barbara has two years seniority.

• *Work setting:* Aircraft plant.

• *Example of problem:* Working side by side on an airplane assembly line takes patience and tolerance. Hours are demanding and deadlines emotionally consuming. Barbara frequently lets Paul know he is not carrying his share of the load. She perceives him as lazy and out for easy money.

Paul has a different perception. He feels Barbara has a need to exercise authority she does not have. Even though she has two years experience on him, he does not imagine her as a co-worker. He dislikes Barbara's air of wisdom, marked by the decided age difference. He feels she assumes a "mightier than thou" attitude and under no circumstances will she relinquish it. Paul perceives that Barbara does not consider him to be an equal.

• *Efforts made to resolve the problem:* Paul feels he has tried to express his deepest frustrations to Barbara. At times he has shown anger. He has told her he will involve their supervisor if she doesn't modify her superior behavior. She simply maintains her authoritarian pose by threatening to expose his ineptness on the job. Paul is working at not allowing her attitude to control his personal feelings or job performance, but finds it difficult.

Case 3: Circumventing the Boss

• *Problem area:* Bruce views his authority challenged by Jennifer's circumvention activities.

• *Type of work relationship:* Bruce is Jennifer's boss.

• *Work setting:* Insurance agency.

• *Example of problem:* Bruce has fifteen women working under his supervision. He is in charge of a large insurance agency's business office. He believes himself to be a fair business manager, allowing his staff special privileges and occasional tardiness.

Jennifer wants a promotion within the business office. She is assertive and, according to Bruce, hassles him continually about a raise and a different position. He has taken a firm stand. He does not believe she is deserving of a higher level job.

To complicate the matter, Bruce's boss, the insurance company's general manager, has been brought into the picture by Jennifer. She has complained to him of unfair treatment within the business office. Bruce is angered by this blatant circumventing of his judgment and authority.

• *Efforts made to resolve the problem:* Bruce does not want to terminate Jennifer. She is a productive and energetic worker. He also does not like her overzealous need to secure a higher paying position, even at the expense of usurping his authority. He has attempted to support her enthusiasm, but at the same time has been critical of her tactics. He has encouraged her to follow the chain of command and trust his judgment and timing concerning a possible promotion for her. Success at resolving the conflict runs in cycles.

You will note that the preceding examples were situations involving men's efforts to interpret the authority question as challenged by women. Let us now cite three examples reported by women. Many problems were sent to us in the area of authority; the following are the most glaring.

Case 4: Earning Respect

• *Problem area:* Patricia sees Jim as untrustworthy, controlling, and condescending in his relationship to her.

• *Type of work relationship:* Jim is Patricia's boss.

• *Work setting:* A medical educational service.

• *Example of problem:* Patricia is a licensed airplane pilot. Her boss, Dr. Jim, flys his medical equipment from one hospital to another, testing patients, and educating hospital staffs. Patricia's job requires her to be on call for emergency and planned flights. During trips, Dr. Jim makes innuendos about her flying ability. Sometimes he sends her back alone while he takes a bus. His messages are subtle and his excuses for not always flying with her are flimsy. Patricia feels her boss is a jerk. When she confronts him with her feelings, he pretends there is no problem. To complicate matters, Patricia believes she has to earn Dr. Jim's confidence continually, especially in her ability as a pilot. She doesn't know how to do so.

• *Efforts made to resolve the problem:* Patricia has requested numerous hearings with Dr. Jim to express her feelings of anger and frustration. She knows her flying position is of ultimate importance in the success of the medical business. She wants praise, not criticism. When Patricia and Dr. Jim talk, she does not trust what he says. He only pacifies her with statements like, "Don't worry, everything is okay," or "Just relax and do your job." Patricia's fear is she won't be respected as a good pilot. It is a given fact her efforts to succeed as a female pilot are constantly met with male dominance and mistrust. If she quits flying for Dr. Jim, her chances for similar pilot positions are minimal. Remaining in her present situation provides minimal rewards.

Case 5: Gaining Acceptance

• *Problem area:* Donna feels unaccepted as an equal by Jack, even though both are in positions of equal status and responsibility.

• *Type of work relationship:* Donna and Jack are peers.

• *Work setting:* University.

• *Example of problem:* Donna and Jack have taught in the same psychology department for six years. Jack has fifteen hours more of graduate study than Donna. During the past year she has experienced him as arrogant and unaccepting of her ideas. When they have team-taught, Jack has undermined Donna's concepts and dominated the lecture. In department meetings Donna watches Jack intellectualize and seek control of the agenda. When she suggests he should be more open to her ideas, he responds with psychological jargon, suggesting she is a weak and needy person. She suspects he believes she is inferior because she is a woman.

● *Efforts to resolve the problem:* Donna feels discounted by Jack because he won't accept her as a peer. She has told him how she feels, but instead of acknowledging her and offering to renegotiate a change in their relationship, he continues to view her as just another angry woman and a troublemaker.

Donna changed her strategy. She wore more professional type of clothing, lowered her tone of voice, but kept her assertive stance. She viewed his need for peer authority over her as basically his problem. There is now new evidence of respect.

Case 6:   Difference in Style

● *Problem area:* Nancy's style appears to be misunderstood and unaccepted by the men she supervises.

● *Type of work relationship:*   Nancy is a district attorney, working with a group of male law enforcement officers.

● *Work setting:*   Law enforcement office.

● *Example of problem:*   Nancy's predecessor was a strong, paternalistic man. His style of managing was dominant and flamboyant. He had the attitude that "no one can do it as well as I can." Nancy, however, has a style that is more low key and reserved. She believes that people are responsible for their own actions. She trusts her abilities and skills, but has had difficulty establishing her credibility with these men. In fact, she's overheard them saying, "Oh, she's just a woman and we don't have to do what she says."

Since Nancy wants to be respected and taken seriously in her position, she decided to assert her power. After reviewing the problem with her boss and agreeing upon a strategy, she called a meeting of these men. She reviewed her job description and responsibilities as well as theirs. She stated her views on management style. She confronted them with her perception of the problem they were having with her and indicated that none of them could afford to waste time in these past uncooperative efforts.

The risk Nancy took paid off. By bringing the problem out in the open, she won the respect of enough of the men who agreed that they needed to work with her so all of their work could get done. Slowly but surely she is gaining the acceptance of her total work group.

Different Problems—Different Solutions

The problems men and women cited seem similar. They are. Either can feel victimized by the other as a result of a misunderstanding concerning power and authority. Helplessness sets in as one tries to seek compatible solutions with the other. However, the victimizing has different roots and different manifestations. Our research indicates that men assume the positions of authority, even though they may have a woman superior or peer. Just because they are male, regardless of job status, men act superior. It is a basic premise, based on gender. The question is, how can a woman legitimize her position of power, knowing that anything she attempts may not make a difference?

Efforts women made to resolve the authority issue ranged from earning to demanding respect. Our research shows that neither approach works without a loss of integrity. It seems futile for women to seek understanding in relationship to men around the authority question, especially on the job. All the guidelines for agreement lack the needed impact. For instance, in seeking work equality women can avoid argumentation, adopt conflict-reducing techniques, fake anger, "humanize" the opponent, and minimize the distortions. However, the problem is so deep, surface attempts seem out of place and often ineffective. Are there any solutions for men and women who want to survive meaningfully where authority is the issue?

We have hinted that answers to such a question are often virtually absent. When viewed from an historical point of view, this may be true. If, however, we place confidence in a person's capability to change and not be controlled by the past, the following ideas may prove to be valid possibilities. We are suggesting some ways the question of authority in the work place can be addressed openly and practiced fairly. Here are some ideas.

1. Provide opportunity in mixed groups for men and women to tell their experiences in earning, using, and fighting for authority. This is called synergism—the combining of energies to discover new possibilities and disprove the myths. It happens best when women and men discover together, not perpetuate confusion separately.

2. Clarify and restate the authority that comes with your position. Review your job description and areas of responsibilities with your boss

and then with your subordinates. It helps to confirm the support that your boss will provide while you try to establish respect from others. When the situation calls for you to use your authority, do so firmly, without apology.

3. Determine your style of dealing with authority. Learn as much as you can about why you behave as you do, where your stress points are, and what your strengths are. Study various models that describe management styles, such as Hersey/Blanchard's "Situational Leadership Model," or Blake and Mouton's "Managerial Grid." Select the aspects of these models that are most compatible with your value system and the demands of your kind of professional work. Then practice this chosen style consistently, so those who work with and for you can depend on a pattern of behavior from you.

4. Don't let the past control the future. Even though images of how women and men are supposed to behave may have roots in history, write your own future. Set the example by your behavior, raise questions, join forces with others who want to control their destinies too. Take the risk, but don't wait until you have all the answers. You are on the cutting edge of change.

5. Assume that the system in which you work must be examined if these authority issues are to be resolved between men and women. Study how organizations function. Elicit the help of professionals in organization development who can help assess your place of work and implement needed changes.

Remember, there are no easy answers around male-female struggles for earning and keeping authority. Authority has always been and will always be a major issue. Encounter the issue at its roots. It will be hard work. It may even be rewarding.

5

WE'VE GOT TO STOP MEETING LIKE THIS!

Meetings are an integral part of our work lives. Whether or not we like to attend meetings and whether or not they produce the results we want to achieve, the facts are that we must attend and lead an amazing number of them and for many years.

A man, on the average, spends forty-three years of his life in the workforce compared to twenty-five years for a woman. However, when a woman isn't being paid for her work, most likely she is involved in community activities that also call for frequent meetings. Doyle and Straus in *How to Make Meetings Work* claim that an adult spends an average of four hours a week in meetings.[1] We calculated this to represent 874 days of one's life. Now if the working man or woman is in middle management they can plan on spending one-third of their time in meetings, or an average of thirteen hours every work week. Moving up to the executive suite means even more meetings—approximately 50% of the work week, or twenty hours.

[1] Michael Doyle and David Straus, *How to Make Meetings Work* (Chicago: Playboy Press, 1977).

Not only do these professionals attend many meetings, but, judging from comments we heard, many of these meetings are unsatisfactory and unsatisfying. We asked the women to focus on some specific aspects of meetings with this question in mind: "Have you ever had a problem in meetings convincing others of your ideas, sharing power, or receiving recognition of your abilities and skills?" Sixty-six percent answered yes.

The men were asked, "Have you ever had a problem in accepting women's ideas, sharing power with them, or giving them recognition for their abilities and skills?" Seventeen percent admitted they had.

Although "meetings" represented the second-most frequently mentioned problem for women—second only to authority—when they were asked to indicate how serious the problem was, 29% said it was a major problem, whereas less than 1% of the men considered the problem serious.

Their responses prompted us to inquire into what kinds of problems women have in meetings and how meetings can be more productive and meaningful for the participants. We found two aspects of meetings often caused problems: (1) People: Who's coming? Who's committed to its purpose? (2) Process: What happens in the meeting? What roles do members play?

PEOPLE

Who is coming to the meeting? Who is invited but doesn't come? Who is not invited and why? Experts on meeting planning such as Doyle and Straus outline criteria to use in determining who should attend: 1) involve those who are affected by a decision; 2) include the decision-maker; and 3) periodically bring in someone new. But these authors do not tell readers what to do when difficulties occur such as those described below by three different women.

Laura shared the following with us: "I'm the first woman in management level working for my newspaper. Every week the men hold a meeting to set goals for the week, but somehow they consistently 'forget' to invite me." This is a common complaint among women who have moved into a high level in their organization and find themselves in a numerical minority. "If I'm not included in these meetings, how can I make decisions and know about essential information and plans?" asked Laura.

Another middle manager, Ruth, in personnel, wrote us about how the "Good Old Boy Network" ignored her when hiring decisions were being made. She said, "Administrative decisions on selecting new employees, definitely a part of my job description, were being made by a group of older men in the company, including my boss, and I had no recourse after the decision was made." Perhaps these decisions were made in formal meetings to which they "forgot" to invite Ruth, but more than likely they were made in informal settings—"huddles"—in someone's office or over lunch.

Letty, a supervisor in education, said that she calls a meeting of her professional peers for a certain time and place. At the appointed time few show up. This pattern repeats itself, and she doesn't know why when even with the authority of her supervisory position her peers do not attend.

We believe these three cases illustrate the problem of perception of the worth of the individuals who were not included and of the prestige of the person calling the meeting. In the first two examples, others (bosses and peers) discounted the importance of Laura and Ruth, so they were "forgotten" when invitations were issued and "forgotten" when the men huddled to consider the merits of a candidate for a job. In the last case Letty's peers probably did not perceive her as important enough in the organization's informal power structure, so her meetings were ignored.

Assuming that the goal of these women is to be taken seriously and thus included in decision making, what could and what did they do? None was very successful initially. One did nothing, which, of course, perpetuated the problem. The newspaperwoman reviewed the problem with her boss and indicated that her effectiveness depended on getting the information dispensed at these weekly meetings. In essence, Laura invited herself to the meetings. Her presence was not questioned, but then she had to deal with a new problem because they wanted her to take the notes!

The educator found minimal success when she personally contacted each person after her agenda was distributed. However, attendance improved when Letty involved her peers before she published a completed agenda.

Since it was the women who indicated the attendance problem to us, we realized that the men were unaware of the extent of their exclusion of women. With this reality in mind, we are suggesting the following options to individual women facing this problem.

1. Be assertive about being included in meetings. Let your boss know why you need to attend certain events. Be alert to when and where they are held. Attend uninvited, assuming you have weighed the risk of that choice.

2. Set up clear expectations from the beginning. State it more than once if necessary, but start the new job or first meeting you hold with the ground rule that everyone is expected to attend. When this is not observed, talk about the problem openly in the next meeting. Elicit the cooperation of those who attend to resolve the problem. We heard of some fun consequences placed on the latecomer. Wear a dunce hat for the meeting. If late three times, you must bring brownies to the next meeting. And the next time, the latecomer would automatically be the secretary.

3. Take every opportunity to educate your male colleagues and bosses. Call attention to their behavior. Give examples. Educate, do not attack. One woman told us that at first her private conversation with a male didn't appear to accomplish much, but later he even called and apologized.

PROCESS IN MEETINGS

Even with the correct composition of people in a meeting and a well-prepared agenda, the dynamics of the meeting itself can undermine its outcome. We found that the process of meetings caused the greatest number of problems between men and women.

Men and Women in Groups

Researchers have observed the behavior of men in all-male groups and the behavior of women in all-female groups. Natasha Josefowitz lists two key differences including: (1) An atmosphere of camaraderie is achieved by men through joking and discussion of events. Women do this usually through discussion of self and family. (2) Men tend to compete for power, whereas women are more likely to collaborate and try to please each other. On the whole men were more impersonal and indirect, addressing remarks to the group as a whole rather than to individuals. Ninety percent of the time women addressed individuals and personalized their remarks, speaking for themselves.[2]

But since the focus of our book is to explore what happens when men and women work together, let us look at what other researchers have observed happens in mixed groups. Men shift their attention and remarks from the group as a whole to individuals; women direct their remarks to the more dominant (and powerful?) men. Competition, the basis of the all-male group, increased among women in the mixed group as they vied for the men's attentions. Women's talk decreased and they asked fewer questions. What about personal gain? Data showed that in all female groups women learned more, whereas men learned more in the mixed groups.[3]

Typical Roles in Groups

But these general statements do not help the individual man and woman solve the specific problem they face in meetings. So let us look at roles people play in groups. Which behaviors in a meeting interfere with its purpose and outcome?

Tables 5-1 and 5-2 outline the basic task and maintenance roles people may assume while in a meeting. However, there are both helping and hindering behaviors demonstrated by participants. It may be helpful to you as you read over these roles people play in groups to check those that you recognize as the ones you most frequently use.

As you might expect, it was many of the hindering roles that were mentioned to us as problems for men and women in meetings. However, as Table 5-3 indicates, there can be problems when some of the helping roles are either over or under used.

Most of us recognize that men generally utilize the task roles and women tend to use the maintenance roles. We can trace the cause of this to the intense socialization process that taught men and women to act according to their sex roles. Therefore, we behave in groups and in especially rigid task and maintenance roles, according to our preprogramming.

[2] Natasha Josefowitz, *Paths to Power* (Reading, Mass: Addison Wesley Publishing Co.), p. 178.
[3] Ibid., pp. 177-79.

Are We Satisfied
with Defined Roles?

Are we satisfied with these defined roles? Evidently, not always. Businessman Irv admitted that sometimes others told him he emphasized the task roles too much at the expense of some of the maintenance roles. Nonetheless he, somewhat defensively, judged the women in his work group as "overly social" in their behavior.

Jane, a businesswoman, disliked having to shift her roles according to the composition of the group. In mixed-gender groups she usually listened; in all-female groups she was comfortable initiating information and contributed more fully.

Frank, a mature government official, complained that his female subordinate, Claudia, constantly wanted him to take her side in any discussion, to defend her against attacks from the male-dominated meetings, and generally "to fight her battles."

Each of these professionals recognized the roles they were playing in meetings and how some of these roles were nonproductive. Their self-awareness of this was the first step toward deciding whether or not to continue behaving the same way in the future. Irv did not change his behavior, partly because he was not ready to make an honest evaluation of his own style. Rather he chose to divert his attention to the women's styles. Jane increased her effort to contribute useful information more frequently. Frank counseled Claudia, discussing methods she might use to respond more constructively toward those who would attempt to "put her in her place" in the meetings.

When group members collectively recognize that rigid role playing can inhibit the decision-making process, then more progress can be made. We heard of several cases where staff members routinely rotated the key roles of chairing the meeting and taking notes so that the roles would not be assigned or assumed merely on the basis of gender.

Responses to Ideas

Next, let's look at some all too common responses when ideas are presented in meetings: interrupting, passive waiting, discounting, and outright ignoring. As we'll see, each of these behaviors is another inappropriate use of roles by group members.

TABLE 5-1 Task Roles

HELPING		HINDERING
INITIATOR: proposes task or goals; defines a group problem; suggests procedure or ideas for getting the task accomplished.		WAITER: waits for others to initiate action, offer opinions or facts; answers when asked.
INFORMATION OR OPINION SEEKER: requests facts; seeks relevant information about a group concern; asks for suggestions, ideas or opinions.		AVOIDER: remains oblivious to the task or problem, shows no interest in seeking additional information other than her own.
INFORMATION OR OPINION GIVER: offers facts; provides relevant information about group concerns; states a belief; gives suggestions, ideas or opinions.	TALKER: engages in excessive talking about her own ideas; interrupts others	(or) WITHDRAWER: removes self psychologically or physically from the group; does not talk.
CLARIFIER: interprets or reflects ideas and suggestions; clears up conclusions; indicates alternatives and issues before the group; gives examples, defines terms.		IGNORER: remains unaware or unconcerned about confusion of others; ignores any disagreements and doesn't seek to clarify anything that might lead to conflict.
SUMMARIZER: pulls together related ideas; restates suggestions after group has discussed them; offers a decision or conclusion for the group to accept or reject.		MOVER: charges ahead before checking for readiness to summarize or closure.

TABLE 5-1 Task Roles

(continued)

HELPING	*HINDERING*
CONSENSUS TESTER: checks with group to see how much agreement has been reached and how ready the group members are to consider a decision.	DECIDER: without checking with group, makes the decision that enough discussion has occurred and that it is time to reach a decision; values efficiency and speed in deliberation.
NAVIGATOR: keeps group members on the set agenda or tasks, draws attention when off course.	PLAYBOY-PLAYGIRL: regards the meeting as a social occasion; acts as the jokester; pokes fun at other members and helps everyone have a good time.
RECORDER: writes down suggestions, makes a record of group decisions.	
ARRANGER: prepares set-up of room, passes out materials, refreshments; operates equipment.	

© Lois B. Hart *Moving Up! Women and Leadership* (New York, NY: AMACOM 1980)

TABLE 5-2 Maintenance Roles

HELPING		HINDERING
ENCOURAGER: is friendly, warm, and responsive to others; accepts others and their contributions; regards others by giving them an opportunity to contribute or recognition.		COLD SHOULDER: is unresponsive, unfriendly toward others; generally ignores contributions of others.
HARMONIZER: attempts to reconcile disagreements; reduces tension, helps people explore their differences.	(or)	CHALLENGER: incites conflicts among members, "needles" and irritates others for own sake; uses emotionally charged words and sarcasm, puts down others' ideas.
FEELER: expresses group feelings; senses feelings, mood, relationships within the group, shares own feelings with other members.		FEELER: expresses a feeling about every idea, suggestion, or problem, usually with a great deal of emotion; may also try to psychoanalyze and unveil others' feelings.
GATE KEEPER: helps to keep communication channels open; facilitates the participation of others; suggests procedures that permit sharing remarks.		BLOCKING: disagrees and opposes beyond "reason," resists stubbornly the group's wishes for personally oriented reasons; uses hidden agenda to thwart group progress.
COMPROMISER: when own ideas or status is involved in a conflict, offers a compromise which yields status; admits error; modifies in interest of group cohesion or growth.	CONFORMIST: always agrees with whatever the group wants, smooths over any conflict.	CAUCUS FORMER: seeks out one or more other supporters to support own special needs regardless of the group.

TABLE 5-2 Maintenance Roles

(continued)

HELPING

STANDARD SETTER AND TESTER: checks whether the group is satisfied with its procedures; suggests new procedures when necessary.

GROUP OBSERVER: keeps watch on how the group is functioning, what helpful and hindering roles are used; periodically gives a report on observations.

© Lois B. Hart, *Moving Up! Women and Leadership* (New York, NY: AMACON 1980).

TABLE 5-3 Over- and Under-Used Roles

MAINTENANCE ROLES				TASK ROLES			
HELPFUL		HINDERING		HELPFUL		HINDERING	
Women	Men	Women	Men	Women	Men	Women	Men
Encourager, harmonizer, feeler, gate keeper, compromiser	Compromiser	Conformist, feeler	Challenger, blocker, caucus-former	Information- or opinion-seeker, clarifier, recorder, arranger	Initiator, information- or opinion-giver, summarizer	Waiter, avoider, withdrawer, ignorer	Talker, mover, ignorer, decider

Interruptions. It wasn't difficult to find examples of this pattern. A particularly astute elementary school principal admitted he formed his own opinion before his female subordinate had a chance to present the full picture. A middle manager in a hospital noted how her boss consistently listened with only "half an ear." A professional counselor in a community college told us how her male colleague was always interrupting her to make his point even when the other members of the group were still interested in her presentation. He would say, "I have a better idea. . . ."

As we were gathering this information we discovered other researchers—Candice West and Dan Zimmerman of the University of California at Santa Cruz—were studying the patterns of men interrupting women versus women interrupting men in both personal and work settings. Their preliminary results validated our observations: Men tend to interrupt women sooner than women interrupt men. In their study men interjected after twelve syllables, whereas women generally waited until twenty-five syllables had been spoken. They believe the repeated interruptions give women the impression that their ideas are not as important as men's.[4]

The problem of interrupting, in relation to our earlier description of roles people play in meetings, is an example of the overuse of the information- opinion-giver and talker roles by men and the overuse of the waiting role by women. Excessive giving of information and talking leads to domination of the group. Men often fall prey to the overuse of these roles by talking on and on about either the topic at hand or extraneous items. If interrupted, they may maneuver the focus back to themselves in order to continue talking about their own ideas and thoughts, obviously believing that what they have to say is *more* important than what others have to say.

Another form of interruption occurs when the individual ignores an established agenda and begins talking about his problem or project. Jack told us about a pattern he notes in staff meetings he attends that are chaired by a woman. Two of his colleagues continually divert the conversation to their interests. Jack felt that the chairwoman merely needed to re-assert the agreement the group members had made about what would be covered in the agenda, in which order, and for how much time. With a tightly controlled agenda she could gently lead the discussion back to where it belonged. Jack felt that his colleagues' behavior was an attempt

---

[4]Candice West and Dan Zimmerman, NBC: *Today,* 1980, interview.

on their part to show up the woman and that she needed to demonstrate to them and others who was in charge.

Overuse of the Waiting Role. When women and men sit and wait, they can play right into the hands of the dominating members of the group, who will interrupt, present their own ideas and opinions, and generally influence the group's actions. All too often women overuse this role. They sit back, listen to others, formulate an idea in their mind, but think, "Oh, it's not such a good idea," only to discover that the same idea presented by a colleague is well received.

Waiting is often caused by a lack of confidence in one's ideas and one's right to express them. Perhaps, also, the woman has been interrupted, discounted, and ignored enough in the past that she finds it easier to wait, hoping someone will ask her opinion.

Jack, the same astute observer of his colleagues, told us that what bothered him about this waiting behavior of women is that it isn't until later, long after the meeting, that he finds out what they wanted to say or were dissatisfied with. "Why don't they say what they think in the meeting? It isn't fair to complain later if they choose to be silent in the meeting," he commented.

To resolve this "waiting game," we suggest two techniques: (1) Set up the ground rule that each person will speak for one to three minutes on the issue at hand. No one else may interrupt until the round is completed; and (2) Divide the group into triads, or buzz groups, discuss the topic for five to ten minutes, then return to the larger group and report their findings. These methods ensure that both talkers and waiters have "air time."

Discounting. Once again, it was women who complained, "My boss asks an inordinate amount of questions concerning the validity of my statistics and even dismisses the issues as unimportant. He relegates my topic to his 'can wait list' when it is really important he deal with it now." Another woman said of her boss, "He uses meetings to discredit my technical ability; he'll tell me publicly that my concern is irrelevant." A third woman said of her peers, "They [peers] caused the most problems for me, especially those who really don't know me or my skills. They disregard my ideas and suggestions."

Being the recipient of discounting is upsetting enough when one person is making a verbal attack, but imagine yourself in Juanita's position, as told to us by a supportive male peer. She is director of accounting; her colleague, Wayne, is director of purchasing. Each were presenting reports of equal value to a dozen other directors. His went unquestioned. However, as soon as Juanita finished, all ten other directors began questioning her report. The supportive male said, "The questions weren't just for clarification purposes, they were actually attacking!" What especially amazed her peer was that she received no support—neither from Wayne, nor from the other two women directors.

This pattern of discounting others' ideas may be an indicator of the overuse of the challenging role, one that many men fall into. Men, more often than women, tend to ask why, a form of a challenge that often elicits a defensive response.

Juanita and Wayne didn't like the outcome of the meeting, so later they reviewed the incident in private. They diagnosed the directors' behavior as a challenge to Juanita's competence. To alleviate her defensiveness and to change the dynamics, they brainstormed some alternatives, listed below.

1. Do not name call. Responding in kind never works.
2. Try humor. Although an effort, Juanita came up with this humorous response to use when colleagues challenged her: "Goodness, I see I've been taking all of your attention. I want to share it with my colleague, Wayne, and let him get a share of the limelight."
3. Talk with the directors individually after the meeting to determine what really is the problem they have with Juanita. This conversation could be initiated by Juanita, by her boss, or even by her supportive colleague.
4. Preplan the presentation with Wayne more carefully. Decide that both of you will introduce the report as a team effort and field questions together.
5. Discuss the conflict with the chairperson of the meeting. Ask that next time this happens, the questions be directed to the content of the report and not at the individual who is reporting.

Ignoring. Another form of discounting a person and her or his worth is to completely ignore them. Typical was this comment given by a female government manager: "The worst 'putdown' of all is when my boss ignores what I say, almost like I wasn't even there." Perhaps you have heard the claim that the opposite of love is not hate but being ignored.

Sometimes women use the ignoring role in combination with their conforming role. It most frequently occurs in a meeting when the woman denies the value of her idea and readily agrees with the group. Or she may ignore her "intuitive feeling" and say nothing.

What to Do?

What did these professionals do to counter interruptions, discounting, and ignoring on the part of those with whom they worked? One woman indicated she spends excessive amounts of time verifying her facts and figures to ensure credibility in the meeting. Another person met with her male boss privately, discussed her perceptions and elicited his promise to take her more seriously. A third person went to her boss's superior with the problem.

In groups, leaders can establish ground rules as to how discussions will be handled. As mentioned earlier, control over who talks and how long one talks often eliminates these problems quickly.

Individuals are learning how to interrupt the excessive talker in a constructive way. They interrupt and state their own opinion or idea clearly and firmly. Each time their idea is discounted or ignored, they repeat their behavior until they are no longer ignored. By so doing they are demanding equal time.

But in the cases we cited above, the degree of success depended on the degree of awareness of the parties involved regarding the fact that the roles they were playing interfered with the meeting's success. Researchers West and Zimmerman also found it is an unintentional and unconscious behavior, thus men especially must learn to recognize their tendency and to monitor their roles.

Begrudging Acceptance

The first response to an idea can be, "I don't like it so I'll discount or ignore it." The second response can be just as distressing—"I will accept it, however, begrudgingly."

How will you know if this is happening to you? Most people (women, in particular) said they just seemed to know; they intuitively felt their ideas were threatening to or were resented by others. They received little enthusiasm, although there was tacit agreement. Unfortunately, begrudging acceptance was later manifested by resentment emerging in other forms of sabotage, such as backhanded comments, poor or late attendance at future meetings, and general "footdragging."

Resentments and defensiveness are difficult to pinpoint. However, both must be dealt with if men and women are going to be more effective with each other. One woman supervisor, Katherine, knew her presence was resented by the older men. She persisted, continued to attend the meetings, and held onto the belief that the resentment would diminish with time. Eventually it did. Sonya, a librarian, used her awareness that her competence tended to threaten her peers. She phrased her suggestions in meetings in the most neutral, nonthreatening manner she could think of. She also cultivated informal relationships with each man. Later these tactics paid off in the formal meetings. In fact, she indicated she had a high degree of success using this strategy.

Stealing Ideas

Another tactic, opposite to ignoring or discounting others' ideas, is to find them so appealing, or useful, as to "steal them" for oneself. Unfortunately this is nonproductive and unfair, but it is a common complaint we often heard. For instance, Terri, a mental health professional, told us that Ron, a peer, initially discounted or set aside her ideas, but later on the ideas resurfaced as his own and were accepted readily by others at staff meetings. Terri recognizes that Ron's usurping of her ideas assured her that the ideas eventually would be implemented, but it didn't lessen her resentment. She confronted him with statements such as, "I believe you misinterpreted what I said," or "I don't feel you heard me correctly," as a way to keep this peer, and others, on their toes and aware of the source of the contribution.

Another professional took stronger action and directly confronted the person who stole the idea and related this information to their boss. Margaret had the advantage because her work group had periodic evaluation sessions to review the process used in their meetings. In a meeting Margaret provided feedback on the theft of ideas, which remedied the problem permanently. Another way to minimize theft is to put your ideas on paper and distribute signed copies as the ideas are presented in a meeting or within a follow-up report.

Other Blocks in Meetings

In our experience we have seen meetings flounder and participants unhappy with the process when the following roles are inappropriately used.

Blocking. The primary interest of the person using this role is the pursuit of her or his own opinions and ideas with disregard for the direction the group is taking. The harmony and success of the group is at risk. The attitude is one of "I intend to get my own say." The rights of individual expression here override the group decision making.

Expression of Feelings. The underuse of the expression of feelings in a meeting can keep others from really knowing how an individual feels about what is happening. This is especially hard for men, particularly in a work setting and in a group that is predominately male. On the other hand, the role is inappropriate when feelings are expressed at the wrong time or in the wrong manner. Women who express their hurt through tears may leave the other group members confused and at a loss. Men who express their feelings with anger also create a negative effect. (See Chapter 9 on emotions for a more complete analysis of this problem.)

Harmonizing. The harmonizer role can be useful at times when conflicts need to be smoothed over, especially when there isn't enough time to resolve the problem completely or when the individuals involved are not really ready to deal with the problem. Women, however, tend to misuse this role by prematurely interrupting conflict because of their own desire for peace and harmony.

Decision Making. Movers and deciders also need to learn appropriate timing. A mover decides the group has discussed the topic long enough and is ready for a decision or closure. While she or he may be ready, the group may not be, and attempts to move the group faster can cause resentment and confusion. A decider tends to be overly anxious to finish the talk at hand and becomes restless when she or he thinks enough time has been spent talking. Although attention to elements such as time, decision-making, and adherence to agenda is encouraged, overconcern with them is just as inappropriate as ignoring them.

The Goal

Whenever you call a meeting or participate in one, it is a legitimate goal to expect that the objective of the meeting will be accomplished, but not at the expense of any of the participants. Individuals and meeting leaders can strive to increase the appropriate use of the task and maintenance roles and to decrease the use of those roles that hinder progress.

This checklist of ideas may help you as a group member.

1. *Learn.* Study the dynamics of what happens in groups that function well and that don't. Teach others what you know about group dynamics and how to use task and maintenance roles in the most appropriate manner.

2. *Select.* Of the roles you might play in each meeting, which naturally fit your own style and skills? Decide which are helpful and should be continued. Choose new roles and practice them. Be flexible, use different roles depending on the situation in each unique meeting. Encourage others to use their strengths and to develop less-used roles.

3. *Be prepared.* The more carefully you have prepared any presentation for a meeting, the more likely others will take you seriously and your ideas will be implemented. Many professionals are benefiting from the skills they have learned in giving more formal speeches and applying these techniques to meetings. Their new confidence and presence commands attention—and action.

4. *Assert.* Believe in your ideas and be persistent in presenting them. Think of how much productivity is affected if you do not.

5. *Gather support.* Get the cooperation of the other men and women who attend the same meetings with you to help improve the outcome of future meetings and to eliminate the destructive behaviors reviewed here.

6. *Educate.* Take every opportunity to make those around you aware of what is going on. As one male principal said to us, "How can I determine success [in overcoming this problem] if I'm unaware of what I am doing?" Too few management courses address sexism in group dynamics. So if you recommend men to attend, be sure you know what they will be taught.

If you are a leader of meetings, you have even more opportunity to influence others. Every meeting needs a traffic cop, and the leader may often have to be this person. Who is invited, who gets to talk, who is heard, and who is given credit can all be determined by the leader. Model the behaviors that you want group members to demonstrate. Insist on fair and equitable behavior from your subordinates in meetings. Counsel those who don't get the hint and need the firm hand of guidance.

"We have simply got to stop having meetings like this . . ." and we can.

6

WHAT SHOULD I CALL YOU?

At a recent meeting of 200 women, the new chairperson was being introduced. The outgoing presiding officer was flamboyantly praising her successor, and then came these words: ". . . and so it gives me great pleasure to introduce to all of you our new chair——, our new, uh, our new chair——, our new *chaircreature!*"

A woman in her sixties related that incident to me. She was laughing and crying at the same time. The outgoing chairperson was obviously struggling to be proper in her language. Not long ago, women in leadership roles were called chairmen. Today a new awareness permeates our society. Women are not chairmen. A nonsexist vocabulary is being taught and learned. It is often difficult to practice by both women and men.

Half of the women we surveyed felt language was a problem for them in the work force. Twenty-two percent of them saw it as a major problem. One-third of the men felt that language was a barrier, but a scant 3% felt it was a significant problem. This differentiation adds significance to how men and women interpret the definition of language.

In this chapter we will deal with the insensitivity of language meanings, how women and men approach the language barrier, and the kinds of messages conveyed in terminology. We will conclude with some signs of hope.

THE LANGUAGE PROBLEM

Insensitivity Abounds

Language is an area that is problematic for the supervisor, peer, and subordinate. The causes of the problems are deep since our history has conditioned most men to refer to women as girls or guys, and to men as boys or fellows. Women are also conditioned to refer to themselves as the "girls in the office." One woman commented, "It is especially discouraging when the secretarial staff continues to call themselves 'girls.' Surprisingly, the men in my office seem more sensitive to the issue than the women do." In spite of increased attention in the last decade to the form and meaning of words, simple words such as women and men escape most people's vocabularies.

Women's Approach to the Language Problem

Women in their work settings are descriptively referred to as girls or you guys and are grouped into a category called mankind. Most women feel their efforts to sensitize the office members to a more appropriate description are often met with a teasing, joking response. "I want you guys, I mean you guys and gals . . . wait, let me say it right (sarcastically), you men and women (bowing) to be at the next sales meeting. . . ." Instead of proper language being used naturally, it is tampered with jokingly.

Nancy Smith writes poignantly concerning women and language in her poem, "Call Me a Woman."[1]

CALL ME A WOMAN

I am twenty-five
And when I am called a girl
I speak like a girl;
I flirt and giggle and play dumb.
But when I remember I am a woman,
I put away childish things
And speak out, and share, and love.

[1]Nancy Smith, "Upper Room," Nashville, Tenn. 1976, p. 15.

62

I am thirty-six
And when I am called a girl
I think like a girl;
I feel incompetent
So I serve and help
    the men around me.
But when I remember I am a woman,
I put away childish things
And work, and create, and achieve.

I am fifty-two
And when I am called a girl
I understand like a girl;
I let others protect me
    from the world.
But when I remember I am a woman,
I put away childish things
And decide, and risk, and live
    my own life.

NANCY R. SMITH

Women at work tell us their answer to heightened sensitivity is constant accountability. Persistently correcting the speaker, man or woman, keeps the issue alive and up front. Even a touch of humor may help interpret the seriousness of the language problem. The humor is different from the caustic "being-made-fun-of" type.

Men's Approach
to the Language Problem

The questionnaire responses showed each woman sensitive to not being referred to as a woman. Demeaning language for them was the problem. Interestingly, in their responses men made no mention of feeling personally degraded by a woman's terminology. Instead the men focused on the use of foul language, off-color stories, and obscene subtleties, particularly when uttered by men in the presence of women. Only a few male responses centered on the insensitive use of words like "girl," "gal," or "chick." Such meager response emphasizes the need for education and training, especially for men, in regard to the meaning of guys versus girls, ladies versus gentlemen, and women versus men.

Most men approach the language issue from the exterior, monitoring their swearing and joke telling. The concern is deeper, more internal for women and has historical significances and deep implications. A sensitive male told us "the problem is the way men refer to women, not the way women refer to men." For women it represents an attack on their personhood; for men, it is literally a choice of words.

THREE KINDS OF MESSAGES

The purpose of language is to convey a message. Words carry meaning, but deeper than the meanings are the intentions. We raise the question: What is the intent behind the words?

The Unaware Message

This book is written primarily to increase awareness of the need for equality as well as to help achieve equality for both men and women. Sadly, many men and women relate in unequal ways, believing that this is the way it has to be. No one has ever questioned their behavior or words. A man may call a woman "girl" and give her menial tasks at work because he is unaware. A woman may accept the language and tasks for the same reason. They do not know there can be and is a better way.

In an interview with Lou, former director of a woman's resource center, she spoke of the "unaware message in one's nonconscious mind." We asked her, "How does language affect the professional woman?" She said, "Most people, when speaking, are not conscious of language and its meanings. Both men and women operate out of the nonconscious. The result is power and ownership. 'My girls work for me,' said by a man implies possession. He becomes superior; she is inferior. Actually nonconscious language and unsolicited touching add up to male superiority. We may believe men have the advantage in the working relationship because they hold the power, but in the long run their nonconscious behavior is too burdensome to continually act out. This is why men die earlier. Maintaining power, even in a nonconscious way, is stressful."[2]

The Blatant Message

The sacred texts of history have served as a launching pad for sexist language. In the Koran, the religious text of Islam, are the words: "Men are

[2]Lou Isaacson, Interview, January 19, 1981.

superior to women on account of the qualities in which God has given them pre-eminence."

The morning prayer of the Orthodox Jew is:

> *Blessed art Thou, Oh Lord our God, King of the Universe,*
> *that I was not born a gentile.*
> *Blessed art Thou, Oh Lord our God, King of the Universe,*
> *that I was not born a slave.*
> *Blessed art Thou, Oh Lord our God, King of the Universe,*
> *that I was not born a woman.*[3]

Another sacred book, the Bible, uses such language as: "Then God said, 'Let us make *man* in our image and likeness' . . . so God created *man* in *His* own image; in the image of God *He* created *him*; male and female *He* created them" (Genesis 1:26-28).

In the New Testament are these words from Paul the apostle. "But I wish you to understand that while every man has Christ for his Head, woman's head is man, as Christ's Head is God . . . if a woman is not to wear a veil she might as well have her hair cut off; but if it is a disgrace for her to be cropped and shaved, then she should wear a veil. A man has no need to cover his head, because man is the image of God, and the mirror of his glory, whereas woman reflects the glory of man. . . . For man did not originally spring from woman, but woman was made out of man; and man was not created for woman's sake, but woman for the sake of man. . . ." (I Corinthians 11:2-9).

Paul continues his critical interpretation of Christianity in a letter to Timothy. "It is my desire, therefore, that everywhere prayers be said by the men of the congregation, who shall lift up their hands with a pure intention, excluding angry or quarrelsome thoughts. Women again must dress in becoming manner, modestly and soberly, not with elaborate hair styles, not decked out with gold or pearls, or expensive clothes, but with good deeds, as befits women who claim to be religious. A woman must be a learner, listening quietly and with due submission. I do not permit a woman to be a teacher, nor must woman domineer over man; she should be quiet" (Timothy 2:8-12).

[3] Sandra L. Bem and Daryl J. Bem, "Case Study of a Non-conscious Ideology: Training the Woman to Know Her Place," *Female Psychology: The Emerging Self*, ed. Sue Cox (Chicago, Illinois: Science Research Assoc., Publisher, 1976), p. 180.

These examples, found not only in religious tracts, but in historical documents, literature, films, and television programs, provide historical bonding for the male. The message is not hidden for men or women; men have formed from earliest times support systems based on being the powerful one of the species. Subsequent refinements of language reinforced man's position of power. The majority of women have acquiesced.

Lou relates the first telephone call she received after taking the directorship of the woman's center. A male colleague opened the conversation with "how ya doin' girl?"

Lou responded with, "Don't call me girl, boy."

Her confrontation resulted in stunned silence, but she made her point.

"Would most women call a male colleague and say, 'how have you been, boy?'" she asked.

The blatant language message of power can take another form. Ann was explaining to me how a certain computer system worked. Her boss walked by the office and stopped in to hear what was being said. He strategically placed himself opposite everyone else in the room. Ann continued; a few minutes later her boss took over. Although his language appeared sensitive and well thought out and although he spoke in non-sexist terms, his nonverbal language was not congruent with his words. What initially appeared to be a subtle message was a blatant double message. He used certain kinds of terminology to project himself as an equal, but his attitude was one of superiority and power. As he gained all the attention, Ann faded away, a victim of his manipulative ploy. Also verified, as noted earlier, is the fact that men interrupt women more than women interrupt men. Lou says, "For men bonding is important, and it is seen in their behavior as well as by their language."

The Struggling Message

The setting was a graduate school collegium composed of nine men and one woman and Howard, a male professor. To illustrate material the professor would use male metaphors and the words *he* and *mankind* to mean universality. Each time Howard used such language, Lori, a professed feminist, would correct him. It became obvious that such continual interruptions were hindering the spontaneity of the professor. Once he expressed appreciation for being called on his terminology. Another time he ignored her plea, but corrected his words.

After numerous outbreaks and hostile expressions by the outspoken feminist, the professor literally knelt down before her and said, "I know you are upset by my insensitivity. Many of my woman friends see little hope in my changing. But I am working very hard to be more aware. Remember, Lori, I have spoken these words for many years. I am a very conditioned male. I am doing the best I can right now. I know the non-sexist language; it just doesn't always come out that way. Forgive me, but bear with me."

Howard's message was one of struggle. It is not easy in any setting, and particularly in the work world, to make immediate changes. Women struggle, too. Lou says, "I expect certain kinds of verbal behavior like 'girl' or 'hon' from men. It is harder to take this from women because I have higher expectations from my sisters."

Courage is needed to recondition our language behavior. A man attempting to raise another man's consciousness may be laughed at or he may open himself to ridicule; he breaks the historical bond of power and superiority. A woman, in verbal protest of today's sexism, may be labeled as radical or crazy, and others may ask "why doesn't she just leave well enough alone?"

In one of our research groups we were discussing the issue of language. Did the members of the group see any hope for changing one's awareness? The following responses were made.

"We as women need to walk the fine line of being assertive, but not overbearing. I believe more than a single exposure is needed. When I was referred to on a basketball team by my male coach as a guy or girl, I protested. But what helped was when one of my team players also said something. We were nice, but the coach received double exposure. It takes constant awareness and being assertive about the issue."

"We women must battle the feeling of 'what's the use?' Futility sometimes takes over. It is important to stand up for ourselves."

"As men, bringing the language issue to other men, we may be effective because we have the power. Wouldn't that be something for men at work to bring other men to accountability?"

AN AWARENESS SHAKING

The attempts at language equality penetrate the consciousness of both men and women. All persons need an awareness shaking. Learning can be a struggle that produces moments of futility and anger. It takes time. Idealistically, it would be nice to have men and women be highly sensitive to each other's personhood and act out equality in language and behavior in all areas of their lives. Realistically, the struggle is a long one. Reconditioning one's thought patterns takes time, patience, and persistence on the part of both women and men. In everyday conversation, especially at work, people need to be reminded that it can be either he or she, not just he.

Correcting this long-standing historical problem is frustrating because there are many messages coupled with the reinforcement of time. The work setting poses many barriers to correcting the language issue because the issue lacks importance when compared with everything else at work. Production and maintaining a high profile in the business world easily overshadows the internal problem of the appropriate way to refer to a male or female. The truth is that how one does refer to a female or male may very well affect work production and how the company is seen by others in the work world. Language is symbolic of employee treatment. When treatment is fair and just, word travels quickly. Language equality does take time, but time must not be an excuse for lack of action.

Using the word humankind instead of mankind is a break with history. It is amazing that humans have not realized its negative influence before now. But now that it has been recognized, it must be met head on, tested, believed in, and overcome. We must no longer live out of denial. Instead, we must continuously create situations where nonsexist language is practiced with integrity and purpose. When this occurs, women and men will experience major reinforcing events of equality.

7

HANDS OFF!

It is a startling statistic, but 88% of the working women we interviewed said they had experienced one or more forms of unwanted sexual advances on their job.[1] This is only one survey, but others bear out the facts. The work setting is one of the most inviting places in our society for sexual power to be abused.

In our research, 16% of both men and women felt sexual overtones and harassment to be a problem. The men responded defensively. For instance, one man noted, "I feel a double bind when I say 'you look nice today.' I am often accused of being too aggressive. But if I don't recognize her appearance, I also hear about it."

The women responded from a position of powerlessness. Most said they felt little or no choice in conforming to the "office games." In abstract thinking, all of us have choices, but when a woman is struggling to maintain her job for survival purposes, she may not feel she has many choices. That is the moment her life moves from the abstract to the practical.

[1] "Sexual Harassment: A Hidden Issue," *Project on the Status and Education of Women,* (Washington, D.C.: Association of American Colleges, June 1978), p. 1.

DEFINITION OF SEXUAL HARASSMENT
OR UNWANTED SEXUAL BEHAVIOR AT WORK

To define the sexual overtones that often occur between men and women at work visualize the following scenarios.

Scenario 1. Jessica was informed by her boss that the company was installing a shower in the back room. He suggested that "after hours" she might consider "testing" the shower with him to make sure it was in good working order.

Scenario 2. While eating lunch together Sheila was told by her supervisor that their lunch hours would certainly be more exciting if they "put a little spice" into their time together. When she asked, "what do you mean?" her supervisor said, "meet me at the Hilton tomorrow noon and I'll explain further."

Scenario 3. After completing her graduate training, Melissa was selected to do further research at an Institute for Interpersonal Relations. While being interviewed by the committee, it was suggested to her on two different occasions (in private) that she "practice" her interpersonal relationships before departing to the institute for study.

Scenario 4. The organist of a large local church was informed by the senior pastor that he would like to be more involved in the selection of the Sunday morning hymns. When she agreed, he intimated the best time for them to talk about such matters would be in his office late at night, so they would not be disturbed. "The hour didn't disturb me," she said, "rather, it was his look of seductiveness that surprised me."

Scenario 5. Sue was called into her boss's office. He said, "You have been here for three months now. I find you a most attractive young woman. In fact, I would like to spend some time with you—away from the office. I know I am a married man, but my wife and I aren't getting along very well and haven't for years. Besides, Sue, a little extra activity on the side can't hurt you around promotion time!"

These scenarios point out two facts concerning sexual harassment and unwanted sexual behavior. First, it is both subtle and blatant. Second, it is usually initiated by the man. In a newsletter from the Michigan House Committee on Constitutional Revision and Women's Rights, it is suggested that "any workable definition of sexual harassment must include not only continued verbal innuendoes or overt sexual commentary but also must include continual intimate physical contact and possible forced sexual encounter."[2]

To elaborate further, the Sexual Harassment Task Force of the Michigan Women's Commission states "sexual harassment is (1) sexual contact, or threat of sexual contact or coercion for the purpose of sexual contact, which is not freely and mutually agreeable to both parties; (2) the continual or repeated verbal abuse of a sexual nature including but not limited to graphic commentaries on the victim's body, sexually suggestive objects or pictures, sexually degrading words used to describe the person or propositions of a sexual nature; (3) the threat or insinuation that lack of sexual submission will adversely affect the victim's employment, wages, advancements, assigned duties or shifts, academic standing, or other conditions which affect victim's livelihood."[3]

One last emphasis in defining sexual harassment comes from the book *Women at Work,* in which the authors write, "first and foremost sexual harassment is a serious form of economic coercion practiced by men who have the power to hire or fire, to grant or deny promotions or raises . . . second, harassment is a power game . . . the key element in all of these situations is not who is boss and who is employee, not who is seller and who is buyer, but who is male and who is female."[4]

THE PREVALENCE OF UNWANTED SEXUAL EXPRESSION AT WORK

Before discussing the dynamics of sexual harassment at work, it is well to note the extent to which it occurs. This chapter opened with the startling statistic that 88% of working women experience some form of unwanted sexual advances, verbally and nonverbally. In 1976, *Redbook* magazine

[2] "Sexual Harassment," *Capitol: Woman,* House Committee on Constitutional Revision and Woman's Rights, State of Michigan, vol. 5, no. 9, April 1979, p. 1.

[3] "Memo of Sexual Harassment Task Force" (Lansing, Mich.: Michigan Women's Commission, Nov. 16, 1978).

[4] Marlene Arthur Pinkstaff and Anna Bell Wilkinson, *Women at Work: Overcoming the Obstacles* (Reading, Mass.: Addison-Wesley Publishing Co., Inc., 1979), p. 132.

surveyed 9,000 clerical and professional women and found that many respondents had experienced overt physical harassment, sexual remarks, and leering, with the majority regarding the problem as very serious.[5] In a study conducted in New York by the Working Woman United Institute, 70% said they had been harassed.[6] Statistics reveal the intensity of the problem.

However, this doesn't mean 88% of working men are sexually abusive or that 88% of all work situations are undesirable. In *Women at Work*, the authors state, "the majority of the men in the country are fine people who are dedicated to their families and concerned about doing a good job at work. But that still leaves many who are not."[7]

For the purposes of this book we are concerned with the male-female sexual exchange. However, harassment is also very possible within the realm of male-male relationships, female-female relationships, and female-male relationships.

An Interview

Donna graciously, but painfully, allowed us to interview her. She had been employed three years in an accounting firm, staffed with ten women and two men. As is often the case, the men were partners and owned the firm. Donna's position was a staff accountant. Here are her comments.

"It was a crazy place to be. They (both male partners) told me I had all kinds of authority, but it always seemed to be based on my response to them. We would often eat lunch together. When leaving the restaurant one of the guys would say, 'Do you want to pick the hotel or should I?'

"Sometimes in the middle of my working day one of them would 'kiddingly' write me a note suggesting we take a break and 'go make love.' They were very outfront with their message, even though it would sound like a joke.

"One of the bosses, who was recently divorced, played the 'ain't it awful' game. One day he would make up stories of how he was so deprived and starved for sexual involvement, and the next day he would brag about all the women he had escorted to bed. I knew he was just trying to get me

---

[5] Claire Safran, "What Men Do to Women on the Job," *Redbook*, November 1976.

[6] "Sexual Harassment: A Hidden Issue," *Project on the Status and Education*, p. 2.

[7] Pinkstaff and Wilkinson, *Women at Work*, p. 129.

sexually involved. I think he also wanted me to believe he was attractive."

Donna breathed deeply as if in distress, and continued. "Both of the partners continually asked how my marriage was going. Eventually they would get around to my sex life with my husband. I knew what they wanted.

"Other things they did were joke about how well the new help fit on their laps, suggest putting a one-way mirror in the women's bathroom, argue which of the two of them had the prettiest clients, and suggest to all of us women that business would pick up if we slept with the male clients."

We asked Donna how she handled her bosses' behavior. "Personally, I made a joke out of it. I would say things like, 'I wouldn't go to bed with you if you were the last guy on earth.' Or I would be just as crude with them as they were with me. I was not easily embarrassed, but they really tried to intimidate women."

But as the interview continued and Donna's feelings began to surface, it became apparent it was not a matter left at work and forgotten. "Sometimes I would go home and let it all out on my husband. I would tell him what I wished I had said. I would be so angry. I found myself practicing what I would say to them and then go back to the office and fall right back into the same traps. Sometimes I think I encouraged their behavior by not taking a harder stand. I had heard men treated women this way at work so I just thought it was normal. I would be afraid I'd lose my job. I was caught in a bind. I needed the job, but I didn't need all the other stuff that went with it."

Who Are the Likely Candidates?

Donna's experience vividly points out the problem. She was vulnerable to sexual harassment. *Women at Work* points out characteristics found in some women in the work settings that often render them as candidates for sexual harassment.[8]

1. The woman who is timid or insecure about her abilities, particularly as she tries to compete with a man. She can be harassed out of intimidation rather than attraction.
2. The educationally restricted woman who works up to her capacity, but sees limited possibilities for advancement. She could be convinced that complying with the harasser will increase her chances for a better position.

[8]Ibid., pp. 138-39.

3. The woman who accepts the definition of female as primarily that of a sex object. She has a belief system that she is bound by duty to "go along."

4. The powerless woman who works for a powerful man. She feels replaceable and may compromise herself sexually for the sake of work survival.

5. The woman who is head of her household or economically dependent. Most divorced, separated, never married, or widowed women can not afford to leave their work. Her paycheck is her security and often she will rationalize her sexual behavior as a way of maintaining some security for the household.

6. The woman in sales who is pressured by clients to meet sexual demands in exchange for business. Her support system wanes when she has an employer that insists she "comply" or be fired. If she is self-employed she still questions her survival monetarily.

7. The up-and-comer whose ambition makes her a threat to less secure men. Harassment is used by peers to "put her in her place," intimidate her and squelch her advancement.

The Issue Is Power

Sexual harassment, or unwanted sexual behavior at work, boils down to one concept—power. Underlying all the responses women made to us in our research was their sense of futility. It doesn't matter who is boss or who is subordinate, the issue remains one of man assuming the rights of suggestion and coercion. The expectations are unspoken. Compliance yields to power, which is the one element present in all abusive relationships, whether domestic, social, or work related. When power takes the form of harassment, it is an insult. It attacks the very core of one's dignity. It is a political tool, a means to prove "maleness," a means to eliminate competition, and a means to degrade the opposite sex (mostly women).[9] Sexually harassing behavior can potentially occur in a context where there is an exchange of goods for services. "This means settings wherein one individual can reasonably be assumed to have power over another. This power may be in terms of giving grades; or it may be in terms of providing evaluative information to another's supervisor. The 'power' in fact, may just be one individual's ability to make another's life miserable while the victim is attempting to accomplish assigned tasks."[10]

[9] Ibid., p. 137.

[10] Capitol: Woman, State of Michigan, P. 1.

WHY THE WORK SETTING
IS AN INVITING PLACE
FOR UNWANTED SEXUAL ADVANCES

We have alluded to some of the dynamics that occur and promote sexual harassment at work. Here are a few more.

Daily Involvement Breeds Familiarity

Being in a work setting six to twelve hours a day pushes people together, often whether they like it or not. Expecting to see one another on a regular basis becomes a welcome habit or a challenge to be in contact in a new and different way.

A Common Cause

There is a saying that the best of friends are two people who dislike the same person. They have a cause. This is also true in the work setting. Employees, management, staff, and professional or nonprofessional persons get enthusiastic about one another when involved in a common cause. As energies get charged, sexual overtones may take root.

A Convenient Place

Work is often a spilling ground for one's emotions. The boss senses one of the employees is "down." He invites the distressed person to talk about the problem. Soon there is a caring that feels vastly different from anything she's received from her husband or man-friend. Such acts of involvement may be license for more interaction, thus going beyond the bonds of a sensitive boss being supportive to a hurting employee. What began as an act of caring is now interpreted by the boss as "she wants more from me." The employee's response turns from hope to fear. The involvement is no longer mutual.

Expectations

Many times all the cards are not placed on the table at the time of the interview. Thus, false expectations may be assumed by both employer and employee. "I didn't know catering meals at the hotel also meant catering to his sexual whims later," or "I was hired as a computer analyst not a mistress."

A Bribe

When one is desperate for a job and a paycheck, it is fertile ground for unethical demands. An administrative assistant in a federal government agency lost her job after refusing her boss's sexual advances.[11] It has the flavor of a bribe. More blatantly stated, "if you don't go to bed with me I will see to it you lose your job." Another example, in an educational work setting, occurred in California. A senior communications major at one of the state universities told the California State Legislature in 1973 that she knew of "at least fifteen professors who offered students A's for sex."[12] Being vulnerable and desperate are ingredients that promote bribery.

WHAT CAN BE DONE ABOUT UNWANTED SEXUAL ADVANCES OR HARASSMENT?

Most researchers are very good at pointing out the problems, but not as adept at providing the answers. In the problem area of sexual harassment, however, we do believe there are some solutions to the problem.

Challenge the Myths

Myths surround and cloud the issue of men and women at work and their sexual impact on each other. The following are myths—untrue statements. Recognize and challenge them.

[11] "Sexual Harassment: A Hidden Issue," *Project on the Status and Education,* p. 2.
[12] Ibid., p. 2.

Myth: "The woman asks for it—she dresses in an inviting manner."[13] This is a common conclusion drawn by the harasser. It is also a rationalization that promotes harassment and retards solutions. Although there are individual cases to the contrary, limited studies available do not support a woman's dress style as a promotion of "she asked for it."

Myth: "If a woman really wants to discourage sexual harassment, she can do so; if she is harassed she must have asked for it. Many men believe the old saying that a 'no' means a 'yes.' "[14] "No" means "no" and it may need frequent repeating.

Myth: "If a woman ignores it—it will go away."[15] Our research discovered this to be a strategy employed by many working women. The results are minimal. Harassment may continue or become worse when the ignoring tactic is utilized, resulting in a challenge to the competitive side of the male.

Myth: "Most charges of sexual harassment are false. Women will make the charge to get back at a man with whom they are angry."[16] This is generally untrue. Most women realize the risk of public scrutiny, especially if the charges are unfounded.

Myth: "All men in a work setting are sexual harassers—I can expect it to happen to me." Not true. There are an abundance of ethical and decent men in our work society. They are not abusers or sexual opportunists. They have a commitment to family and often see their work as a place to express their talents openly and with integrity. This is the kind of male who sees and treats a woman as a unique person first and as a female second; this type of man is genuine and can be trusted.

In challenging the myths about sexual harassment at work, women must quit absorbing all the blame. "As long as women continue to allow themselves to be made to feel guilty, there will be no impetus for men to behave otherwise."[17]

Know Your Legal Rights

Many courts have not come to terms with sexual harassment as a prevalent and long-standing legal issue. Title VII of the Civil Rights Act does prohibit

---

[13] *Capitol: Woman,* State of Michigan, p. 1.
[14] Ibid.
[15] Ibid.
[16] Ibid.
[17] Pinkstaff and Wilkinson, *Women at Work,* p. 135.

employment discrimination based on sex. While several lower courts have ruled harassment a violation of Title VII, others have disagreed. This causes ambivalence and anxiety on the part of the one being harassed. However, weak as legislation and litigation may seem, there are at least two loopholes that work in favor of the one experiencing unwarranted sexual advances. First, an employer is obligated to investigate any or all complaints of sexual harassment and to deal appropriately with the offender. "When an employer has knowledge that a supervisor has conditioned an employee's job status on a favorable response to sexual demands, and does not take appropriate action, the employer is in violation of Title VII."[18]

Second, one has a better court case if one's job is in jeopardy as a result of not complying with the harasser's demands. Any time a "term and condition of employment unlawfully based on sex" is implied, the court will hear the complaint. The difficult question for the Supreme Court seems to be: "Is the sexual harassment merely the attraction of one person to another, thus making it a private and personal matter, or is one's term of employment based on sex the key issue?" At any rate, harassment of any degree needs the attention of the employer and the legal system.

Establish Policies

If you are employed in a work setting where there is no clear policy of protection against unwanted sexual advances, then help to promote such a policy. Two men in one of our small research groups suggested that women be clearly apprised of their work rights. Education is one key. Having the courage to carry out the rules is another key to controlling the people at work who fall into the category of the harasser.

Therefore, two areas are important. First, establish a clear policy prohibiting sexual harassment, and second, develop a grievance procedure to deal with the complaints. Any time you bring your objections to sexual harassment into the public arena, support for policies will likely be the result.

[18] "Sexual Harassment: A Hidden Issue," *Project on the Status and Education,* p. 4.

Seek Support Systems

As mentioned in the chapter on language, men have bonded themselves together for years. Cohesiveness can be important for women, particularly in the work setting. As one woman said in an interview, "I protect myself. I keep my office door open and I stay behind my desk." But an open door and a desk barrier may not be enough to ward off unwanted sexual behavior.

Support systems, garnered from both trusted men and women at work also protect women from harassment. When unacceptable sexual behavior is experienced by an employee, she has only to call on her "colleagues opposed to inappropriate sexual advances" for support. Knowing there are people "out there" or at a nearby desk may give the needed strength to survive sexually inappropriate advances.

It takes commitment to form such a system of mutual support. However, a sexual harasser may think twice before advancing if he is aware of the support system that offers strength in the office setting.

APPEAL FOR A RENEWAL OF SEXUAL SACREDNESS

Our last solution may sound idealistic, but we offer it to you. As men and women we must treat our bodies as unique and sacred, even in a work setting. This means sexual involvement by invitation only. Sexual harassment is an invasion.

We propose reviewing some basics. Employers and employees may need education in proper office etiquette and behavior. The work setting is a better place to develop healthy relationships when unwanted sexual advances are eliminated.

8

HANDS ON!

We asked over 500 working persons, "Have you ever been excessively distracted due to sexual attractiveness by a boss, peer, or subordinate?" Seventeen percent of the women answered yes; 32% of the men said yes. Both men and women, 17½%, felt this "distraction" was a major problem in the work scene. Later we sat and listened to a select group of people talk about sexual attractiveness on the job. During the conversation, one of the women said, "This issue is terribly complicated. The answers are not always clear or the circumstances well defined."

In this chapter we will interpret the difference between sexual attractiveness and sexual harassment; why men see sexual attractiveness as more of a problem than women do; and ways for persons to avoid setting themselves up for sexual involvements while working together.

THE DIFFERENCE

Sexual harassment can take many forms—subtle, overt, or coercive. It usually has the ingredients of power and manipulation. Sexual attractiveness differs because it involves an intentional choice on the part of both women and men. To be more definitive, note the further differences listed in Table 8-1.

TABLE 8-1

	SEXUAL HARASSMENT	SEXUAL ATTRACTIVENESS
Control of Outcome:	More male dominated	Shared more equally
Rules:	Unequal to both	Followed more closely by both women and men
Threat to Position:	Maintaining a work position a key issue	Not a key issue
Focus:	Dwells more on an act	Dwells more on an emotionally inclusive relationship
Pervading Mood:	Accompanied by a sense of fear	Controlled anxiety and pleasure

MEN'S VIEW

Recall the twelve problems listed in Chapter 1 and their ranking of intensity. Each problem, with the exception of sexual attractiveness, is perceived as a greater concern by women than by men. Our research points to the factor of control when men and women endeavor to reach across their differences in the work place. In all the problem areas, except the one in question, men are and have been traditionally in control, such as etiquette, language, emotions, inappropriate sexual behavior, meetings, authority, work motive, expectations, opportunities, separating work from home, and benefits. But mutual sexual attractiveness in the work setting is different. The control factor rests as heavily with the woman as with the man. This is why we believe the men we surveyed indicated that it was a problem.

Recently at a civic group noon meeting, a male speaker was presenting his ideas about sexism. He traced the origins and the present-day dilemma faced by women and subsequently by men. The all-male group was attentive, but emotionally restless. It was apparent they were not in full agreement with the speaker's interpretation of men's suppression of women in most areas of business.

At the conclusion of the talk, questions and statements came rapidly from the group. "Why do you believe women have little responsibility for the ways things are today?" "Don't tell me women are without power!" "Equality won't work; women depend on men. Men must remain in control and be the key decision-makers in our society."

The speaker fielded each question sensitively and then offered this equalizer to the group: "Do you men really believe you are controlled in your personal or professional life by women? Isn't it true that we as men just verbalize statements of powerlessness, but know differently? The one area of our lives in our business relationships with women that has equal power is our mutual sexual attractions. Women, unless they are being harassed, have as much to say about our sexual involvements as we do."

This is the reason we as researchers believe men see sexual attractiveness on the job as a bigger problem than women do—it is the one area where men experience a lessening of power.

HOW PRECARIOUS SITUATIONS DEVELOP

As noted in the chapter entitled Hands Off!, the work setting is a prime place for sexual behavior to develop. In most work settings an individual spends almost half of his or her five-to-six-day week in the presence of co-workers. Unless the situation is deplorable, the work atmosphere often becomes a supportive place.

Most men and women do not enter the work setting with sexual motives. Sexual attractiveness is the by-product of people being together for the common task of work productivity. So what are the dynamics that occur between two people that detour their work energies to energies of mutual attractiveness? In our research most of the responses to the foregoing question were from men. The following three situations are typical.

The Friendly Persuasion

Skip spoke of working in an office with sixteen women and five men. The overbalance of females seemed to promote "my awareness of the opposite sex and I found myself continually being attracted to this woman or that one, until one day I just got carried away with my emotions."

Skip depicted his marriage as being shaky at times, but not in trouble. His attractiveness to Jan, his colleague, and her positive response was more than he could handle. He began making excuses, as did she, to consult one another on insignificant matters. They began sharing lunch together regularly. Their work lives were being threatened constantly by their sexual and social drives to be near each other. "I would go to the office early so I could be with Jan. Our work became an excuse to be together legitimately. We were so obsessed with each other that we ignored everyone else. The whole office probably knew what was going on, but we just didn't seem to care."

The Traveling Saleswoman

Dan's marriage was tolerable at best. He and Faye went to a marriage counselor but the results pointed to a dismal future. They decided to separate for a set period of time. During the separated months they each saw others socially with the intention of having other companionships but not deep involvements.

Faye was a clothing representative, traveling three days a week throughout the state presenting her lines of clothes to various departments. In one large city she called on the store division manager, Ron, who also happened to be a good friend of the family. He and Dan were former classmates. Faye presented the clothing line, interspersed with comments about the struggle she and Dan were having. The consoling she received from Ron soon led to deeper caring, and without any apparent intent to become sexually intimate, Faye and Ron were physically involved. The business setting had provided the scene for mutual sexual sharing.

Most of the case studies presented to us for this chapter depicted involvements between peers. However, in a few situations, mutual attractiveness transcended the usual behaviors between a supervisor and a subordinate.

The President

William, the president of the company, personally interviewed and hired new personnel. His approach was friendly, open, and caring. When Elizabeth finished her appointment with him she not only was pleased to receive the work position, she also liked William's personal approach toward her.

In subsequent weeks Elizabeth would pass William in the office, reach out and touch his arm, offer a friendly word, and go on. The encounters became more permissive and frequent; touches became hugs and hugs led to suggestive caresses. William's strength—his openness and ability to reach out—was quickly becoming his weakness. Interestingly, as the word spread throughout the office about William and Elizabeth, other women saw such an example as a license for permission, and began pursuing William also. The business became a place to play sexual games; production took a nose dive.

SEXUAL DYNAMICS

What are the dynamics involved in each of these situations? Are there common threads that lead to precarious sexual involvements at work? The answer is yes. Let's explore the possibilities and see if any of them apply to you in your own work life.

1. In each case we have described, both the men and women allowed their body chemistry to rule them. The choices for involvement were intentional and emotionally calculated. It was false to say, "It just happened. I don't know how I got involved; but I did. It was beyond my control." Such a rationale is only an excuse for what later could be called poor judgment and irresponsible decision-making.

2. In many situations the lack of sexual discipline suggests that work is of secondary value and one's sexual desires of primary value. Work commitments find their test of strength when challenged by outside influences, such as depression, lack of enthusiasm, jealousy of a co-worker, or sexual diversions. If an employee lacks the commitment on the job at the outset, he or she might be easily diverted. The extras become the driving forces, and the work is relegated to second place. If you find yourself in such a situation, we suggest you re-evaluate your commitment. An honest appraisal may prevent this diversion.

3. Another commonality that was present in each of the cases was the lack of threat each person felt. When one is being sexually harassed there is the element of inequality and threat. In mutual sexual compatibility this element is muted or not immediately apparent. Both men and

women stimulated each other through their physical excitement. The message was clear—in all three cases participation was mutual. The work setting once again provided the time and space for two persons to express their excitement and pleasure to each other.

4. Deception binds couples together. Most sexual affairs are not public. It takes energy to secretly plan and carry out a sexual involvement, especially in the presence of several employees. Work disguises the involvement; discretion becomes an act of wisdom. A couple experiences cohesiveness through the common sexual bond of deception. This dynamic is often more powerful than the sexual attractiveness itself.

5. A somewhat different but closely related threat that weaves in and out of sexual attractiveness is the power of ownership. When the deception no longer works and the truth is out about Skip and Jan, an irrational strength often emerges that says, "Yes! We are involved! That is just the way it is." Acknowledging and owning the sexual attractiveness becomes an act of mutual strength. It has the same effect on the couple as the dynamic of deception. The difference is that now everything is out in the open. When others find out, the dependency between the lovers increases.

AVOIDING SEXUAL SETUPS

It is important to reiterate we are not disaffirming ourselves as sexual persons. Rather we are dealing with inappropriate sexual behavior at work. We affirm our sexuality; we question the relationship of sexual involvement and work productivity. The following are suggestions of several possible ways that bosses, peers, and subordinates in the work scene can avoid sexual involvement.

1. *Be direct.* When sexual attractiveness begins to happen between colleagues at work deal openly with it. This is not as easy as it sounds simply because most of us have learned to play games rather than to be directly honest. If William and Elizabeth (see the section called The President) would have communicated their sexual feelings at the outset or even when they seemed out of hand, their relationship might have been different. Being open and straightforward doesn't guarantee a lack of sexual involvement, but it certainly offers a dimension of integrity—the first step to a solution.

2. *Identify boundaries and rules.* Closely related to being direct and using "straight talk" about one's sexual feelings is the need to identify the rules. People need limits in which to operate. Skip and Jan (see the section on The Friendly Persuasion) allowed themselves so many sexual liberties in their work setting that their own personal boundaries and limits were abandoned. When two people allow the sexual roller coaster to gain uncontrollable speed, it is most difficult to establish boundaries.

Some companies already have a written rule about work performance with an implication to keep intimacies in check while on the job. Other work settings indirectly suggest principles about work relationships. When the rules are already established, persons have a sense of awareness of their company's expectations. What is accepted, tolerated, or unaccepted is known. However, and unfortunately, most places of work operate out of assumptions. It may not be acceptable if two employees become sexually involved, but no one really knows that until after the fact.

Such ambivalence of rules makes it all the more important for persons, when first aware of another's attraction, to establish their limits early. An example of such rule-setting might sound like this, "Jan, I think we need to be honest about what's happening between us. I know my work performance is only mediocre because of my preoccupation with you. If we don't quit our involvement here at work I might lose my job. We must decide what our relationship is going to be here at work and away from work."

Skip is then seeking to set the rules. He is not denying his feelings; only trying to keep them in perspective with his work responsibilities.

3. *Affirm the attraction, but reaffirm other commitments.* Our findings have been clear about the honesty of feelings men and women experience in mutual sexual attractions. Denial of such feelings only adds another problem. However, the moment of truth often occurs when one has to weigh the circumstances and decide if he or she really desires to devote large amounts of energy to a relationship, when there are other commitments that are also very important. People are often attracted to each other at work for reasons not immediately identifiable. Other aspects of one's life begin to take a subordinate place. One's marriage or children become less of a commitment. The work load is diverted. Friends seem unimportant. Community responsibilities lose their sense of interest.

To affirm one's feelings for another employee is being open and honest. To allow that relationship to be all-consuming is unhealthy. It is necessary in maintaining one's sense of balance—socially, sexually, and emotionally—to keep affirming relationships and commitments. Reaffirmations may lead to a manageable relationship.

4. *Know your motives.* This is simply an act of integrity and self-awareness. A person involved with another, especially in the work setting, needs to make a strong self-assessment to determine motives. Questions such as the following need addressing.

    a. How much do I really like this person with whom I am involved?
    b. Have I been seduced into a relationship because it is the thing *not* to do?
    c. What am I going to gain from this relationship?
    d. Is my work production suffering as a result of my involvement?
    e. Am I creating a situation at work that I may later regret?
    f. Is my willingness to be diverted caused by my low commitment to my job?
    g. Is there a lack of purpose and excitement in my life, which causes me to be susceptible and vulnerable?

Such questions may not have clear answers, but they are worthy of consideration. Self-confrontation is not always easy. Motives are not always readily discernible. Sometimes another party can assist in the sorting-out process. Penetrating questions asked by a trained clinician may illustrate the deep reasons for the involvement. Resolutions may thus come quicker and more easily. That is precisely the reason some companies employ on-the-job counselors.

5. *Choose different behavior.* We make choices to be in relationships. We can also make a choice not to be in a relationship, especially if it creates problems. We often forget we have a will we can exercise as a responsible decision-maker. When one's life becomes complicated because of personal involvements at work, plus the work load itself, it then seems wise to choose a different path.

EQUALLY IMPORTANT BUT SEPARATE

There are hopeful indicators to this very complex issue. At play are two major dynamics: the need to work and the desire for sexual fulfillment.

When one infringes on the other, negative energy begins to flow. When work and sex are kept separate, one's life is more manageable. As George, who works with several women daily in his middle-management position, said to us, "Sure I feel sexual tensions at work. But I have learned to be open and candid about my feelings. Our work environment is a healthy one. We are committed to keeping relationships in a proper perspective."

9

PLEASE DON'T CRY

Chris had worked in her new job for six months, and it was time for her performance review. Chris worked in an almost totally male association, except for the clerical staff and the professional librarian. She had tried hard to start off on the right foot with her peers and boss. She listened a lot, observed the unwritten and stated expectations, and dressed conservatively.

Paul, her boss, outlined in minute detail all that Chris was doing wrong—She didn't joke enough, she was too serious, her clothes were too feminine, she offered her ideas as though she thought she was showing off her knowledge. The litany continued. Chris felt hurt, then angry. How could these criticisms matter? What about her efforts to accomplish what was required on the job description? As Paul continued, Chris felt the volcano of emotions rise. She gulped back her erupting emotions but soon they overflowed. Tears trickled, then poured. In embarrassment, Chris excused herself and left. Paul sat stunned and confused. What should he do now?

Chris called a woman friend and poured out her anguish, both at the negative feedback and at her emotional outburst. Julie's response was, "But, Chris, it's all right to cry. You had a reason to feel hurt. Don't you feel better?"

Chris and Paul are legitimately confused. On the one hand, psychologists tell us that tears and other expressions of emotions are healthy. Joyce Brothers, in a recent article, reviewed several researchers who validated this position. Biochemist William Frey believes that tears have a physiological function, ridding the body of excessive chemicals. Dr. Brothers points out that people who do not express their emotions are less likely to develop themselves as fully; their continued suppressed anger can lead to depression or alcoholism and can result in poorer interpersonal relations.[1]

On the other hand, men and women have been taught from childhood which emotional expressions are appropriate for them. Women are encouraged to "have a good cry and you'll feel better." But they are caught in a bind when their tears appear in the work setting. Men are taught to suppress all emotions and so they are caught in a bind when they counter their conditioning.

Our research started out by exploring how men and women experience this problem of emotional expression at work. After we present those findings, we'll see how men and women are trying to modify the rigidity of their upbringing. We explore the question of what is the appropriate form of expression at work for the boss as well as the employee, and we establish a model for your consideration.

WHO EXPERIENCES THE PROBLEM?

When asked, "Have you ever had a problem expressing your emotions with your boss, subordinate, or peer?" 53% of the women and 26% of the men said yes. Although men and women experience the problem to different degrees, it is a problem worthy of exploration.

IT'S NOT OK!

Figure 9-1 shows what happens when a human being faces a problem that is frustrating, upsetting, or disturbing. One way emotions are expressed is

[1] Joyce Brothers, "Quiz on Emotion," *Times-Call*, February 7-8, 1981, p. 10.

with tears. Feelings of anger are then provoked by a particular incident. But underneath both the tears and the anger is the hurt that is the root of the problem.

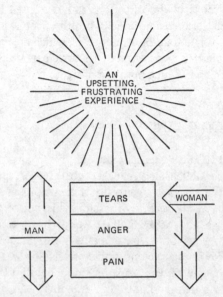

FIGURE 9-1   Male Versus Female Expression of Emotions

We think the model shown in Figure 9-1 can help us better understand this issue of male versus female expression of emotions in the workplace. Our observation is that women seem to be "stuck" at the level of tears as their usual style of emotive expression and men seem to be "stuck" at the level of anger. We do not suggest that either form is good or bad, rather that men and women have been taught to behave in limited patterns.

Growing up male in this culture meant that boys were told that crying was for "sissies" and for girls, but not for them. "Control your tears," they were told. Boys were encouraged to express their hurt in "masculine" ways by yelling, punching, and wrestling—all expressions of anger.

Growing up female in this culture meant that girls were condoned for crying when upset and were even told, "How cute you are when you cry." Girls found tears acceptable and even useful if they wanted to manipulate the men in their lives. On the other hand, "little ladies do not get angry."

By adulthood, males and females were locked into rigid patterns that dictated the most appropriate expression of their hurt. Men and women need to move in the directions as represented in Figure 9-1 (see arrows) in order to become emotionally healthy people. Men need to move down into their pain and up into their tears, which are an alternative form of emotional expression. Women need to move beyond their tears to their anger and to the pain in which both are rooted.

BUT I WANT TO CHANGE

Let us look at two professionals who did try to alter their conditioned styles of expression. Michael, a manager with the aerospace industry, told us about his attempts to be generally more expressive. He consciously worked at showing his feelings—matching his body language with his words, with smiles, and with an alert, attentive expression. But during a course on interviewing skills, participants were videotaped, and he was shocked to see how impassive and nonexpressive he was on the television screen. And he thought he was displaying more emotion!

Tina, a dedicated computer programmer, had also been making efforts to modify her expression of feelings. But in her case, she wanted to control her tears while at work. Most of the time she was successful; but occasionally, she said, the incident provoking her anger was intense enough to cause a volcano of tears to break loose. Once the pressure would build to that point, nothing was going to stop her tears.

Obviously, simply willing a change in one's behavior isn't always successful, at least not immediately.

NOW YOU'RE THE BOSS

To complicate these dilemmas, add the role expectations that come with being a boss. The working leaders with whom we spoke found themselves under even more pressure. Many told us they first experienced the role conflict when given their first supervisory position. Susan wrote, "Upon taking over as the department supervisor, at first I depended heavily on my subordinates—people with whom I'd worked as a peer. Quickly I discovered these emotional ties backfiring. They didn't want a buddy; they wanted a boss. So I had to create a new, personal distance, asserting my professional and positional role. I especially had to find new outlets to express the feelings that I had previously shared with some of my colleagues."

Generally, we found that these working men and women could not win either way: If they behaved the way they were taught was most appropriate as men and women, it was limiting; if they tried out new ways of expressing emotions, they were judged negatively. We found there are ways out of this dilemma.

DIFFICULT QUESTIONS

Underlying the problem, then, are the questions, "What is the appropriate emotional expression for the work setting?" Who determines what is appropriate? How can the individual increase the comfort level of her or his chosen style of expression? Here are some answers to these problems several individuals shared with us.

Please Don't Cry.   Crying headed the list of the forms of expression of strong emotions that caused the most problems. For women it was showing tears, and for men it was how to react to the tears. Tom, a top government official, talked about his younger female subordinate, who obviously "leads with her emotions." He said, "Lana overreacts emotionally when working with men at her level. Instead of rationally using tact and diplomacy, she relies on emotional outbursts."

Similar comments from other men were: "She is overly emotive. She's so sensitive to criticism, off-the-cuff remarks, and even joking." This reference to a woman's apparent lack of humor often emerged. The men complained that a woman, when faced with a difficult task—perhaps one she is unprepared to handle—often breaks into tears. Sometimes the pressure to handle a task is imagined by the woman. Dan told us he found that his assistant stopped crying when he reassured her that no one was intentionally pressuring her to do the frustrating task in a particular way.

A marketing researcher, Bill, stated that the work pressures he experienced from his boss resulted in emotional responses from her;

whereas he thought that if she would just think things through more thoroughly, her response would definitely be more appropriate for her position and their work setting.

Some organizations have more restrictive norms about the expression of emotions. Nancy's place of work had definite sanctions against the expression of strong feelings. So when the stress increased, she found herself making extraordinary efforts "not to crack. If I show my feelings, it will be seen as a sign of weakness. Once that happens others start to take advantage of me." Leslie was told how "cute" she was when she got angry. This only made her more angry.

It became clear to us the more we discussed these problems with men at work, that it was *their* discomfort with women's style of expressing emotions, especially tears, that was at the root of the problem. Perhaps this is a clue for some solutions. The men were using the only model they knew—the one they were taught from childhood—to assess the women's forms of emotional expression. Their narrow perspective on what was appropriate to express and when and where these emotions should be expressed, explain their unfair judgment of women's behavior. Tears and other forms of emotional behavior were judged by men as wrong.

The "Catch 22" occurs when a professional woman tries to act "more like a man," keeping her emotions in check. Brenda, upon hearing of her selection for a position as a trainer in a national association dominated by males, decided to use this new opportunity to learn from her past work experience when the expression of her feelings was misunderstood. So starting the first day on her new job, Brenda dressed and acted totally professional. "I was friendly, but not overly warm with my colleagues. I never made comments or told jokes that had any sexual overtones. I might have a drink with a small group after work, but only occasionally, and I never invited them to my house." Did her new behavior give her the results she had hoped for? Unfortunately, what she called her "new professional image" was seen as cool and distant by the men. Her boss, thinking he was doing her a favor, took her aside and told her many others found her cool attitude not unlike ice on a mountain. He suggested she joke more with the men, even when the jokes were sexual in nature.

Brenda, thinking this male reaction was unique to her, happened to mention the experience to a woman colleague who worked in a different type of business that was also male-dominated. Brenda, although initially dismayed at her colleague's experience, was somehow relieved to learn that they had had similar situations.

As researchers, we found the expression of emotions a common and frustrating phenomenon for working women. "I'm damned if I do express my emotions, and I'm damned if I don't."

The men interviewed also expressed the frustration in trying to find the right balance in expressing their emotions. Increasing numbers of them are being told by their female co-workers and especially by the women with whom they live that they would be much easier to work with if only they would express their emotions. Even with concerted efforts, such as Michael's, many of the men do not report significant changes in their emotive styles.

We suspect it is because these pioneers are well aware of the sanctions against behaviors that may be construed as feminine. Richard Nixon, for example, upon losing the presidential election in 1960, broke into tears before the press. Can you remember anyone being supportive of him? Instead the reaction was one of surprise and criticism.

We know of a high school principal, Charlie, who was generally very expressive. He would let the tears come when the occasion touched him. Faculty members, students, parents, and other administrators witnessed his unusual display. For example, when confronting a student for disciplinary reasons, he would often cry from utter frustration. When addressing students in assembly his tears would flow easily when describing the students' negative behavior. Such displays of emotions by Charlie were generally perceived as signs of weakness and incompetence.

I'm Angry at You. Most of the men we interviewed chose to use verbal anger other than tears to express the underlying hurt. However, they were often aware of how their anger backfired or produced less than satisfactory results. We noted the frequent cases in which the man who is angry at a woman in a work setting may "pussy foot around," indirectly lodging his complaint. We suspect the reason for this avoidance is a fear of her emotional reaction to his anger. Common responses of women when anger is directed toward them range from passive acceptance to an outpouring of tears.

We have observed that when this same type of man is angry with another man, his response is more direct and more candid. He may even use a joke or a fatherly manner to ease the tension. We believe he uses this style because, being a male himself, he can predict the other man's behavior more than a woman's.

Too often women do not get in touch with their anger. However when they do, the men face a new dilemma: They are again very uncomfortable, but this time it is with the woman's anger, not her tears. The men are left speechless and often more angry.

One educator, Carolyn, described an incident when she met with her two male bosses to try to iron out some problems. As the one boss became more and more angry, she began to express her anger too; this in turn accelerated his anger. Never having seen him so out of control, she decided to leave. With her hand on the doorknob he literally yelled at her, "Don't you dare leave!" Fearing for his health because of his high blood pressure and her own tears that were gathering under the surface, she left until both could regain a calmer manner.

WHAT IS THE GOAL?

Since the expression of hurt leads to better mental and physical health, we can assume that it also leads to more productive employees and more satisfying organizational life. We believe the goal is not to control our emotions but to increase their role in our lives and to identify more outlets for their expression.

Deny or Express? Accepting our own emotions, hurts, pain, disappointments, and styles of expressing them and, in turn, accepting others' expressions of emotions are positive steps. If a person chooses to deny his or her own emotions, then the legitimacy of another's emotions is also denied. If a person predetermines what is the most appropriate form of expression for oneself, then judgment of the styles of others follows as a result.

Outlets. After self-acceptance of emotions comes identification of outlets for expressing them. The outlets suggested here are easy to use. Physical activity was a popular method used by those we interviewed—jogging, biking, racquetball, having fun while sorting out the conflict. Others used a special place, a private room in which to scream, cry, shake, or laugh uproariously. Other people punched away their anger into a bag not used merely to dissipate the emotion, but rather to gain a clearer perspective of it and the situation that caused it.

What's Best? Many times, however, we do not have the luxury of time or place to divert emotional energy. We can, though, review what caused the outburst and analyze its appropriateness. Based on the assumption that we have the ability to control emotional responses, we can select the form of expression that best fits the occasion. Ask yourself these questions as you review your options.

If I use this way of expressing my emotions
1. Is the presence or absence of others beneficial or detrimental to me? To them?
2. Is there sufficient support for me and for them if either of us "gets out of control"?
3. What will be the risk if I choose this expression? Is it a real or imagined risk?
4. What other forms of expression could I use?
5. Has this other person ever experienced this alternate from me or from others of my gender?

It's Too Late! What if you made a poor decision, choosing the wrong time or place for a particular form of expression of emotion? Naturally this happens. Those people we talked with who felt they handled a certain situation well said they followed up the emotional "explosion" with a calm discussion. This allowed both parties to review what happened and to resolve the conflict. They also discussed together their individual reactions to each other's styles of expression of emotion.

It's OK and You're OK. The expression of emotion was not thwarted nor judged when the recipient was totally validating of the emotive person. Several of our professionals indicated their training as social workers, ministers, or counselors taught them useful skills. For instance, when faced with strong emotional outbursts, they automatically accepted the expression with accepting statements such as "Go ahead, I know you're upset," "Tell me more about why you're so angry," or "You're OK." Others found the use of humor alleviated the tension. For example, as tears poured out, a male boss pulled out a box of tissues and said warmly, "Go ahead and cry, there's plenty in the box."

But I'm Uncomfortable. But often others are very uncomfortable with our style of expression. Obviously, we cannot control how others choose to react to us—only how we choose to respond to them. Therefore, these can be difficult situations.

We believe the ideal solution involves modifying child-rearing practices. If parents, teachers, and other adults in children's lives would modify their rigidity concerning appropriate expressions of emotions, the children would grow up to become more mature adult males and females better prepared for life's trials and joys.

While we are waiting for that long-term change to occur, organizations can provide education for employees to help them learn how to expand their repertoire of skills and to increase their understanding of emotions. Classes that encourage acceptance of others' styles are needed. Video tape is an especially useful tool to provide feedback for those trying to modify their behavior.

Wisely Retreat. As we have discovered in the other problem areas at work, many times the best solution is to retreat and explore a healthier place to work. In the case of emotional expression, some professionals told us that the emotional climate of their workplace did not match their own needs. Several attempts were made to be accepted or to modify the organization's norms, but in the end the answer was to leave. It wasn't that the individual's style was wrong; it was that the style was mismatched with the organization. We learned that in each case, the individual wisely used the previous, negative experience to select more carefully the next place of work—one that was more compatible with emotional needs.

Conclusion

Many men and women are learning to express, not bury, their emotions. This is difficult because of the strong cultural messages we have received that dictate restrictive behavior. Each gender group has been rigidly fixed into a pattern as to what is most appropriate to express. However, we believe the price of continuing in the old patterns is too high; instead we must try to expand our forms of emotional expressions.

10

HOW SHOULD I TREAT YOU?

One must question if Amy Vanderbilt did any of us a favor when she wrote her book on etiquette. In the 1950s and 1960s guidelines for women and men in regard to politeness and appropriateness of action were accepted and practiced. Today many of these guidelines are confusing.

In our research of the twelve problematic categories, etiquette ranked seventh for both men and women. Thirteen percent of the males and 35% of the females saw it as a problem. However, only 3% of the women viewed etiquette as a major concern. Such findings raise the following questions: "Has the work world come to a comfortable place around male-female protocol?" "Is the etiquette problem so subtle that people are missing its importance?" "Relative to other problems, is the etiquette question just not as serious?"

This chapter explores the influence of historical etiquette teachings and the confusion such learning lends to both men and women, and it takes a look at a new equality in etiquette. Any hopeful answers found in this chapter lie in our belief that women and men are capable of change and that they will implement such change in both their personal and working lives.

A DEEP PROBLEM

We believe the lack of recognition of a need for equal treatment by both women and men is an indicator of a deeper problem. Unawareness of the messages conveyed through traditionally proper, polite, and accepted behavior perpetuates the inequality. This deep-seated concern was first challenged in the 1960s, especially by women. During this era females gave themselves permission to question their roles. The outspoken ones were considered radical; the quieter protesters were simply tolerated and probably misunderstood. While women were in search for their place, young men were taking dance classes, wearing white gloves so as to not soil the "girls'" dresses, and learning all the right language and mannerisms that suppress equality. It was a confusing time then as it is now. The men of the eighth-grade dance class are still living out their training and not understanding the turmoil.

Of course, the problem becomes confused because of those women who still believe they need "taking care of" and are the "weaker sex." Examine the underlying messages in Ms. Vanderbilt's *New Complete Book of Etiquette*, first revised in 1952 and most recently in 1967. The category is entitled "How Does a Boy Ask for a Date?" (Note there is no instruction on how a young woman exercises the same privilege.) In reference to money and dating, Ms. Vanderbilt notes that many young men incur extra expense or new financial responsibilities when they begin to date. She suggests that if allowance is not adequate to support his extracurricular activities, a young man should get an after-school job. Regarding the "girl's" responsibility, Ms. Vanderbilt suggests she adjust her tastes to the young man and make no financial demands upon him. There is nothing said about the young woman carrying her share of the financial load.

The messages conveyed thirty years ago and lived out today in the name of good etiquette promote unequal behavior for both sexes. It carries over into the work world as evidenced in the following examples.

Out to Lunch

When Mary's boss proudly announced the birth of his first grandchild she invited him to have lunch with her to celebrate the occasion. At 11:45 A.M., R.J., the boss, suggested to Mary they leave work a little early to avoid the noon rush. He proceeded to usher Mary to his car, opened her door, and drove off suggesting they eat at El Macho's, the best Mexican food restaurant in town.

In the restaurant, R.J. courteously seated Mary, motioned to a waiter for assistance, and after a brief conversation about the menu specials ordered for both of them. The meal ended after a pointed suggestion by R.J. that both should return to work. As Mary requested the check from the waiter (after all, she did invite her boss for lunch), R.J. immediately countered her overture with, "The treat's on me!"

"But I asked you for lunch, R.J. I want to pay, please."

"Listen, Mary, that's nice, but I'm not going to let you do that. Waiter, here's the money for the meal, keep the change."

As they left the restaurant, R.J. helped Mary out the door and down the step. Arriving back at work, R.J. thanked Mary for suggesting the lunch together and hurried into his office. The rest of the workday was a very busy one for R.J. and one of frustration for Mary.

The behaviors of R.J. and Mary in the scenario are a result of conditioned behavior. Men and women have been taught particular kinds of etiquette to characterize specific roles. The following questions of role expectations arise as we examine the luncheon closely.

1. Why should R.J. assume leadership and control over the luncheon he was invited to?
2. Is Mary incapable of opening the car door for herself?
3. Were Mary's suggestions considered for a place to eat?
4. Cannot Mary seat herself in the restaurant?
5. Is Mary unable to order for herself?
6. Why wasn't Mary allowed to pay for the meal?
7. Can't Mary go out of the door and down the steps by herself?

WHY DOES IT HAPPEN THIS WAY?

We suggest that the four modes of behavior listed below—familiar to all of us—symbolize the inequalities inherent in the work scene.

1. *Conditioned behavior.* The Amy Vanderbilts in our lives have doubtless been well-intentioned teachers of social and business etiquette, and most men and women in the work force do not question their up-

bringing. R.J. most likely transferred his social etiquette training to his working world. He believes all that he did was proper. Mary is less sure, but she is still programmed to respond in an appropriate way—"like a lady." We are conditioned: To change is a violation of our historical social teachings. Thus, for Mary to open R.J.'s car door or to assist him down the step would be considered silly and inappropriate.

2. *Power and control.* Politeness can be a way of gaining and maintaining control of a situation. When Mary initiated paying for the meal, R.J. immediately took control. He was polite and outwardly a "gentleman." He also usurped her decision. Opening doors, assisting another down a step, seating someone at a table are all acts of good manners. They can also exemplify strength and weakness. In most instances, the man assumes the role of helper and the woman becomes the helpless. It is subtle, but a man exerts power in relationships under the guise of etiquette.

3. *It's comfortable for men.* If men do not view today's etiquette as a problem, how *do* they feel about it? Many say they feel comfortable and secure, since most men believe in taking care of women and being the dominant person. His is a superiority stance. In working relationships men influence decisions and production; they are expected to do so. Why, then, would a man want to relinquish his position of superiority?

4. *It's comfortable for women.* From our experience, review of literature, and current research we believe a majority of women do not wish for equal etiquette; only a minority want change. While men like to take care of women, women like being taken care of. There is definition in both roles; expectations are clear. Women know their place. Such conditioned behavior and mentality is a sad commentary and a hindrance to new forms of equal etiquette. "This is just the way it is" becomes the motto.

It was courageous for Mary to invite her boss for lunch, but there the new etiquette stopped. Every other action that occurred in their luncheon encounter was controlled by R.J. Mary allowed him to take control; she chose to be waited upon. She did not confront him with her own rights of etiquette. She took a secondary position. For both men and women it is dangerous to be comfortable about unequal etiquette, because our conditioned manners will then set in deeper and stay in longer.

A STATE OF CONFUSION

Women and men are at different stages of awareness concerning a definition of equal etiquette. It is new and risky thinking to suggest updating the traditional forms of manners. Remember that working relationships are extensions of social relationships. If men and women are confused socially, they carry this confusion into the world of work.

Amy Vanderbilt devoted a section of her book to "A Man's Manners in the Business World." She stressed that aspiring young executives who wish to get ahead must do more than become expert at their jobs; they must also learn to be adept socially.

Confusion enters the relationship when a woman refuses to be treated as an object. Picture our luncheon tableau again. Reverse the behavior. R.J. invites Mary, his secretary, to lunch. She reminds him at 11:45 that they should go early to avoid the noon rush. She ushers him to her car, opens the door of her car for him, and drives off, suggesting they eat at the Ms. House, a fine restaurant.

In the eating establishment Mary courteously seats R.J., motions for a waitress to assist them, and proceeds to order for both of them. After lunch, R.J. requests the check, only to have Mary say, "No, no. I want to pay." R.J. insists it is his desire to pick up the bill; he did invite her out to eat. Mary counters with, "It's my treat," and gives the money to the waitress. Upon leaving Mary opens the restaurant door for R.J. and takes hold of his elbow to help him down the step, and they return to the office.

Absurd or amusing, you say? Not if one believes in equal etiquette. While both scenarios have a touch of exaggeration, especially the latter one, what is needed to clear the confusion is a fresh model of etiquette, based on equality for all persons. Let us look at what such a model would entail.

A NEW STANDARD
OF EQUAL ETIQUETTE

Here are some guidelines we believe can enhance person-to-person relationships in both social and work situations.

1. *If it's right for you, it's right for me.* Women and men have the same rights. Being polite to one another is a courtesy extended out of personhood, not gender. Tish Baldrige, a business executive, wife, and mother says, "A woman's manners . . . should be just the same as those of a polite man in the same situation. She shouldn't expect people to fuss over her, light her cigarettes, stand when she enters, or that sort of thing. In fact, manners in almost any business situation should not have sex lines. Good manners are good manners, no matter who uses them."[1]

In an interview Margo said to us, "When I am asked to pour the coffee, I say, 'John, I think you are closer to the coffee pot; it is just as easy for you to do it.' In some ways I am educating John to his responsibility of responding just as easily, if not easier, than I am able to respond. In another way I am saying, 'I am not a servant here. We can all pour coffee with equal skill.' Another way of looking at shared responsibility is to become a director in certain situations. As to pouring the coffee, take control of the scene. Don't be controlled; be the director, 'John, I think you are closer to the coffee pot.'"

2. *It is time to overcome gender politics.* What appears on the surface to be simple etiquette may have deep political overtones. The word *power* creeps into the relationship once again. Ohio State University sociologist Laurel Richardson Walum cites the act of opening doors as symbolic of gender politics. Is such a simple gesture a case of simple etiquette? Not always. Patrice Horn quotes Walum, "Opening a door for a woman . . . is in fact a political act, an act which affirms a patriarchal ideology."[2] Ms. Horn continues, "In our society, the person with the authority opens the door; the doctor ushers in his patient; the mother, her children; the boss, his employee; the man, the woman."[3]

In one of our research groups a young man suggested very eloquently, "People should open doors for people, not genders. Our minds have to change so our hearts must take over. If we have to always be political in our relationships of 'who does what for whom,' then we are missing the point of just being in a relationship and acting accordingly because we are not always genders, we are people."

[1] Tish Baldrige, "The Return of Etiquette," *Scoops Magazine,* vol. 1:1, March 1979, p. 4.

[2] Patrice Horn, "Door Opening as a Political Act," *Psychology Today,* December 1973, pp. 39-40.

[3] Ibid.

3. *Women and men, stand up and be counted.* Updating behavior is a mutual responsibility for both women and men. Admitting the uncomfortableness of new manners and equal power may need talking through. There will be struggles, defensiveness, and frustrations. What is important are the lessons that take place. Women and men need to keep one another accountable, particularly in work settings.

Rosalie suggested the concept of rehearsing responses ahead of time. "I prepare my comebacks before I get into any situation with a man. I know it is especially hard to take a stand at work, so I rehearse ideas in my mind. I try to anticipate so I am ready. It works and I feel more able to deal with the various work situations that have potential uncomfortableness for me."

4. *Laugh a little; it hurts less.* Etiquette is a serious matter, but laughter or humor may assist in diffusing its intensity. Tammy told us that when a man at work asked her to get him a cup of tea, she said, "I am turning in my waitress uniform today. Would you care to wear it?" Such subtle humor may begin to heighten one's awareness and assist in putting the etiquette question in proper perspective. Another humorous message was conveyed by Beth who assisted a man off a curb, "You helped me down the last curb, now it is my turn."

Humor has its place and can convey a powerful message. A follow-up discussion will most likely occur, at which time the humor can be interpreted and the etiquette question put into a perspective of equal treatment.

We believe a new standard of etiquette will emerge as increasing numbers of men and women want to change the old ways and try out new behavior. The transitional period may prove to be both exciting and educational. Equal etiquette means recognizing the worth and integrity in every person, regardless of gender. It is starting from the beginning. There are no assumptions of power. Persons need to be treated as persons, not just as genders. Amy Vanderbilt had her day; what she proposed had its place. It is time for a new book of etiquette to be written. And who will be the authors? Today's men and women.

11

GETTING PAID
FOR
WHAT I'M WORTH

A reasonable assumption is that a person may expect and receive money, benefits, and privileges commensurate with one's education and on-the-job experience. But reason appears to have been lost somewhere along the way, because the dismal reality is that this expectation for women at work is unmet.

The men interviewed during our research know this and expressed their concern with a 44% affirmative response to the question, "Have you been aware that women may not be receiving equal benefits, money, and privileges?" Women, of course, are well aware of the discrepancies in the standards of pay and benefits for women versus men.

This problem area—probably one of the most important ones in terms of impact on personal lives—was also the most difficult to study. The roots of the problem are steeped in tradition, and the key to it is economics. The solutions for this problem appear to be far beyond the reach of the dedicated efforts of professional men and women who want to see a change. In spite of the barriers, we tried to analyze the ramifications of this issue as we listened to how it affected the lives of workers, and we offer here the ideas and remedies discovered by the respondents in their search for economic equality.

WHO GETS WHAT?

Even with all things being equal, our studies show that men get more of everything. Perry's experience was typical. Her new promotion to supervisor in a company in the aircraft industry was given as a "catch-up" to match her current responsibilities with increased pay and a proper title. However, even though her education and on-the-job experience were equal to those of her predecessor, her salary was not.

The fact is that American women earn only 59% of what American men earn. Reasons for this imbalance as stated by the U.S. Labor Department include the following:[1]

1. Women are concentrated in those occupations that are less skilled, and thus they are paid less.
2. Women work less overtime than men.
3. Although increasingly better educated, the kind of schooling, training, and counseling women receive directs them into the more traditional female jobs that are, thus, the lower paying ones.
4. Women's pattern of work experience is not as continuous, nor as long as men's.

Ann, now managing editor of a magazine with national distribution, knew that her predecessor earned more four years ago than she does today. Even though Ann's salary had tripled in the four-year period, she wondered if she had a right to complain, especially since her boss does appear to be generous. But Ann's dilemma is typical. How can you ever really "catch-up" if you are given a handicap at the start—a beginning salary that is less than appropriate for the position. Surveys of starting salary offers for graduating men and women of equal education show that men were offered more during their selection interviews.[2]

Base pay or salary for professionals is only part of the benefits package. Margaret, a Christian educator, told us how every job she had held—she had worked for both large and small churches—gave her only a basic salary, traditionally low, and never the fringe benefits of an auto allowance, health and life insurance, or an allotment for further education—fringe benefits automatically accorded to male employees.

---

[1] "The Earnings Gap Between Men and Women," U.S. Department of Labor, Employment Standards Administration, Women's Bureau, 1976, p.2

[2] Ibid., p. 4.

Assignment to office space and equipment was found to be disparate between women and men. Jane noted how her male peer, equal in title and status in their loan company, was given a fully enclosed office while she remains in an open cubicle with other employees in the outer area.

Carrie's office arrangement was especially difficult. For several years she had her own office, but now assigned to a new location in the school district, her office consists of sharing one room with five people and five telephones.

Less tangible benefits, but equally symbolic for professionals, include the degree of freedom they are given and the special privileges they receive. Carrie's experience exemplified this. Originally she managed her own schedule, handled referrals, and made day-by-day decisions. Her new boss now asks her to keep an hourly log of her time, and she must have his approval before acting. These new restrictions are difficult to adjust to, especially when she became aware that her male colleague slides by without this close scrutiny of his daily work.

Another form of discrimination we found was in access to information. Women related case after case when they knew their male colleagues were invited to lunches, golf and poker games, and sporting events—all places where information was shared informally. One day, Kathleen happened to walk into a conference room where five men (her boss and colleagues) were planning a weekend fishing and poker trip. She said, "I play poker, too." They looked bewildered. They, nor their wives, would not have wanted Kathleen along, but she knew how much she would miss because she could not attend.

TRADITION REIGNS

Since the Industrial Revolution, women working outside the home have been concentrated in certain occupations and at the lowest levels of organizations. Except during major wars, positions have been open primarily only in libraries and in teaching, secretarial, and sales positions. Many states passed protective laws excluding women from working under conditions that involved lifting weights or working overtime or at night.

The result of this historical bias and protective legislation was that the majority of women who worked, either full or part time, were at the bottom of the pay scale and thus had little opportunity to receive benefits equal to men.

The men in our research demonstrated sensitivity to these facts, putting their fingers on historical tradition as the major culprit. Ted said it best, "If you are a secretary, you receive slave wages—$1 an hour over minimum. The work is critical and most secretaries do an excellent job. But one hundred women apply for every opening because the hours are compatible with their children's school hours." This pattern assures that future openings will continue to offer less than fair wages.

Tradition also defines the *course* of one's position. Imagine parallel lines: you can enter the job market either on the secretarial track, janitorial track, or the administrative track. Once you begin the course on one track, like railroad cars, you cannot jump the track to another. You are locked into a path.

Janet was perceived as very talented and capable of doing administrative work. Her boss, Robert, was aware that because she was trained as a secretary, Janet had little chance of becoming an administrator. She was in a rigid track.

When Sal, a school administrator, was comparing salaries of a beginning secretary with that of a beginning janitor in his school, he found it was better to start the climb as a janitor. The janitor could start with 12% more wages than the highest classified secretary in the school district.

In the U.S. Government, the defined and rigid civil service classifications mean that you had better know what track you are starting on, because once you begin, it's difficult to change. One case we read about told of a man who started as a Grade 3 mail clerk with earnings comparable to a Grade 4 stenographer. Today the mail clerk is a Grade 31 bureau director earning $14,000 more annually than the woman who advanced only to a Grade 12 principal stenographer.[3]

You may be wondering why we are outlining the plight of the majority of working women who work at the lower levels of all organizations. We believe that the traditions engrained at *this* level have determined the attitudes of all employees and the policies and practices of organizations at *all* levels. A new title on a higher professional level does not guarantee a commensurate benefits package—tradition reigns on.

[3]Phillippa Strum, "Pink Collar Blues," *Civil Rights Digest*, Summer 1980, p. 35.

EXCUSES, EXCUSES, EXCUSES

The facts are dismal: Women receive only 59¢ compared with each $1 a man earns. But surely the higher level professional positions, requiring more education and experience, ensures more equity in pay, benefits, and privileges? Let's see if this is true.

Statistics offered by the U.S. Department of Labor reveal that the educational background of the worker makes little difference—the difference in wages, benefits, and so forth depends on whether you are male or female. In 1974, women with four years of college had lower incomes than men who had completed only eight years of school. With a college degree women received 41% less than men with the same college degree. Ironically, the gap widened between men and women as more education was obtained.[4] Thus men are compensated for the extra effort of going on to school; women are not.

Why and how can this happen? It counters all logic, but remember we are not dealing with logic, we are dealing with money and economics. Those offering explanations—or what we call excuses—reflected the pervasive attitude that a woman's worth is less, thus she doesn't deserve equal benefits.

Excuse 1: "You haven't worked as long." Sandy heard this one when she called attention to the fact that the male colleague with whom she works earns $5,000 more a year than she. The only difference in the qualifications was that he had worked one year longer than she had. She never could understand how one year justified a $5,000 differential.

Excuse 2: "He needs it more." Donna's department head has the flexibility to set the professionals' salaries within an established range. All other variables being equal—performance, education, and experience—Donna receives less than her three male colleagues. The difference? The men each have homes in the suburbs, two or three children, and non-working wives. Donna and her husband have an apartment in the city and no children. The boss perceives that the men need the money more—and they get it.

[4] "The Earnings Gap Between Men and Women," U.S. Department of Labor, p. 3.

HOW MUCH DO YOU MAKE?

A well-kept secret, often difficult and sometimes impossible to learn, is what one's colleagues, bosses, and subordinates are receiving in their benefits packages. Our preceding examples were ones in which the professional had common knowledge on benefits received. Others told us of how difficult it was to get this essential information.

Those organizations, like government or teaching professions, that have a classification system open to public scrutiny would appear to have less opportunity to be discriminatory. However, classifications for grade levels have salary ranges so it is possible to obtain a general idea of another's salary, but not specific figures.

At the opposite end of the scale are those companies that literally forbid employees to talk about their salaries. One scene in the movie *Nine to Five* shows a secretary who was instantly fired for disclosing this information in what she thought was a private place, the women's bathroom. The actual and implied threat exists as a norm in too many places of employment—"You talk or you ask, and you can go looking for another job." This is an effective power ploy to keep employees, both men and women, in line.

EQUALITY UNDER THE LAW

Equality, an American goal since the beginning of our country, is still a reality for only a few. Equal salaries, benefits, and privileges are the desire and right of all women who work, whether professionals or service or factory workers. One strategy that would assist the most people in achieving this goal is to pass the Equal Rights Amendment (ERA). Without the ERA, tradition will prevail and excuses will continue. With the ERA, significant gains can be made to reduce the gap between benefits received by women and men at work. With the power and legitimacy of a federal amendment, every employer must confront the discrepancies, not just those who hold contracts with the government or those who are located in a state that has a statute similar to the ERA.

The Equal Rights Amendment would be the single-most important legal weapon available to eradicate inequality. But it would be more than a legal tool: It would be a symbol of a nation's commitment to regard all employees—male and female alike—with equal rights to opportunity and benefits.

IN THE MEANTIME

Social change occurs slowly and the speed of acceptance of a constitutional amendment is unpredictable. The ERA will eventually pass, but as individuals we cannot control its timetable. We cannot wait for its passage. In the interval, how are professionals currently utilizing their legal tools and strategies?

The Legal Option. A few years ago most women resigned themselves to an inequitable situation. But now many women are using federal and state agencies established to enforce existing antidiscriminatory laws. Some women hold out as long as possible before seeking legal action or assistance. Others give their boss one chance, often seeing through his latest lame excuse, and go quickly to their organization's equal employment opportunity officer, to a government agency, or to a private attorney. The mere threat that an employee might take such an action is often enough for the boss to re-evaluate the situation and make amends.

Some make the tough decision to file a suit, perhaps a class-action suit whose outcome may more broadly affect women's status at work. This route is costly and consumes much energy and time, but successful suits serve as a warning to other employers that the issue is serious.

Become Political. All of these economic issues have a relationship with politics—local, state, and federal. In courtrooms and legislatures decisions are made daily that affect employees' benefits. The government officials who make these inhibiting, or freeing, laws are elected. Therefore, the men and women we talked with give the advice that the more we get involved in politics, the more likely we will be to write our own future. Specific recommendations for action included: (1) monitor upcoming bills; (2) assess the voting records of your representatives; (3) financially support political action committees and organizations who will lobby for your interests; (4) help candidates run for office; and (5) run for office yourself . . . *do something*.

We cannot emphasize strongly enough the importance of fighting for and defending legal, judicial, and political decisions that support the goal of equal benefits for all employees. But in addition to these collective, far-reaching efforts, individuals are also struggling to find answers to these problems within their own departments, schools, companies, banks, and other organizations. Countering the sad statistics and horror stories we heard, however, were some successes.

Stand Up and Be Counted. These success stories involved professionals who held to their beliefs and were determined to reap the rewards of their efforts.

For each woman who said, "I simply can't discuss money with my boss, it's so awkward," we heard another say, "Sure, I'm uncomfortable, but if I don't, who will?"

For each man we heard say, "Why bother fighting for her to get a raise, she's pregnant anyway and probably will leave," we heard another man say, "She deserves the money as much as I do. The outcome of this battle affects me, too."

Men and women professionals are beginning to admit, privately and publicly, that the situation is intolerable. They no longer are accepting the excuse, "We'd like to pay you but we can't and, after all, it's all for a good cause." They are facing up to the fact that money is power, and there is enough to go around. They are refusing jobs if the benefits aren't commensurate with the responsibilities.

The first step is making the decision that your qualifications *are* worth every penny, benefit, and privilege you are asking for. It requires believing in this basic right and "sticking to your guns."

The Door Is Shut and Locked. "We three approached our boss, reviewed how we were receiving more scrutiny on our work than John was. Oh, he listened politely but then concluded that it was not an administrative problem. We three needed to learn how to work better with John." SLAM.

"As director of aquatics, I receive less money and different benefits than the male director of recreation, even though our staff and number of participants are similar. My supervisor said it was up to personnel. Personnel said the job had been properly classified." SLAM.

"When I went to my boss to ask for a higher salary after I learned my colleague was making $5,000 more with only one year seniority over

me, I got nowhere. We talked with the vice president and got nowhere."
SLAM. "So, I'm looking for a new job."

On the surface the decision to quit and look elsewhere may appear self-defeating. However, we found as we talked to so many others in this type of situation that a sane decision is often to admit the door is completely shut and locked and, rather than bang one's head against it, to look for a door more open to equal benefits and opportunities.

Who Else Agrees with You? The second step requires searching for as many other people as possible who might be on your side. Soldiers don't fight a battle alone, and neither should employees. Most likely if you are facing this problem many others are, too, but perhaps they aren't talking openly about it.

Keeping people apart who face similar inequities guarantees that no progress is ever made in eradicating the problem. Professional women are utilizing a strategy actively used by men for some time: "Birds of a feather flock together." Others call it networking. Whatever it's called, use it—invite yourself along on the fishing trip.

Associating in these groups helps you obtain the information you need to determine your next step. Many occupationally based organizations publish results of salary surveys. A phone call to a colleague in another city often reveals salaries offered for your kind of position. Rather than guessing—ask. Rather than getting information secondhand—get it firsthand. It won't take long to find other men and women who believe as you do. It may be harder to find those who are willing to go the next step and fight some skirmishes, but if you don't look, you won't find either.

Prepare for Battle. Similar advice is proposed in other chapters; it holds true here as well. Make your preparations thoroughly and carefully. Storming into the boss's office the instant you learn that your colleague makes more money than you does not usually result in an increase in salary. Instead, based on the success stories we have heard, the plan you devise will need to reflect what you know about your organization, your boss, and yourself. Questions to ask are:

1. What organizational and societal traditions perpetuate inequalities?
2. What facts are available to substantiate the salary other professionals of your education and experience receive?

3. Who else might join you in this confrontation?
4. How many levels of decision-makers are involved in getting what you deserve? How does each one make his or her decisions?
5. How persistent are you willing to be?
6. Can you negotiate well?

Some individuals we spoke to systematically discussed the problem with the boss, then with the boss's boss, and on up the ladder—all in the proper sequence. Others who knew that would not work went directly to the board of directors.

Most employees naively believed, "If I just present the facts, justice will prevail, and I'll get my fair share." They quickly learned how to push back traditions and work around excuses. However, they never did alone what could be done with others, or at least not without the image of having "mythical millions" at their command.

Sometimes persistence is trying. One department head, Anne, waited six weeks between each appeal she made to a new level in her organization. She was the victim of the old delaying tactic: We delay, she waits— and with each delay, she wears down a little more until she drops her demand.

Those who succeeded recognized from the beginning that years may be required to achieve their goals. Yes, *years.* They wisely recognized the potency of tradition but chose to keep chipping away at the wall. The fact that substantive change takes time reinforces our advice to identify who else is willing to go along on the journey. Sustaining momentum is easier when there are backup reinforcements.

The gains made were never as great as desired. Margaret, the Christian educator, achieved moderate success. She received the extra benefits of an automobile allowance and educational training, but no increase in her base salary. However, her actions raised the issues and her successor automatically received these benefits—without a fight.

So, as the catch-up game goes on and on, women may not actually catch up, but the individual at least wins something and her or his successor can concentrate their efforts on new and higher goals.

The Public Is Watching. Another tactic used by individuals is to create public pressure on the organization that is resistant to change. Most are sensitive to community pressure—who wants to look like an ogre? One professional told us how she made the suggestion to a local reporter to study this exact issue, resulting in a series of articles naming companies that were lagging behind. This exposure in a newspaper did more to bring down the wall of resistance than any individual efforts had done.

IS IT WORTH IT?

Changing historical and organizational traditions and finding answers to the economic dilemma require considerable effort. Everyone wins if this issue is resolved. Naturally those individuals who will receive more equitable money, benefits, and privileges will gain the most, but the employer will also profit in the long run because satisfied employees produce more. Yes, the efforts we make to effect economic equality *are* worthwhile.

12

OPPORTUNITY IS KNOCKING —OR IS IT?

"Opportunity knocks only once," is a common saying we have heard for years, and usually it is quickly followed with, "When opportunity knocks on your door, act." Such homilies are passed from generation to generation and eventually become so entrenched in the folklore of the culture that it is difficult to separate myth from reality.

Based on our research we found that opportunity—the opportunity to become whatever you want to be, to obtain increasingly important positions, and to achieve one's work goals—is a reality for men, but a myth for women. Both men and women hear the knocking on their doors, but what they are able to do about their motives to achieve is partially determined by their gender.

As we prepared the questions we wanted to ask our respondents, we made the assumption that the opportunities to reach the next step on the ladder they are climbing or the next stage in their professional development are more limited for women than they are for men. Therefore, we didn't ask the men whether or not they thought our assumption was true—that is, that women have limited opportunities—but instead we wanted to know if it was ever a problem for them to identify or obtain opportunities for advancement of female subordinates. We discovered plenty of evidence from men who, in fact, agreed that women may be hindered by limited opportunities. We learned about efforts men were making to facilitate change in this dismal situation. Of the twelve types of problems we researched, this one category offered the most hopeful trend of all.

What did the men have to say? First, 25% said it was a problem for them to identify or to obtain opportunities for the professional women they knew at work, and 15% said this constituted a major problem. Both of these figures ranked high relative to the other twelve problems as shown in the first chapter.

As we analyzed the information obtained by these two questions, we realized that we initially had limited the definition of opportunity as moving up into a higher position. However, the male respondents addressed the problem of opportunity more broadly than as simply gaining a new job title. They viewed opportunity as opening doors to increased responsibility, obtaining recognition, and gaining professional and personal growth experiences. Therefore, what we will present in this chapter reflects their comprehensive observations and experiences.

Upon analysis we learned that men were also frustrated by barriers to their opportunities. For instance, both were affected by keen competition for job openings. For every advertised position, 100 very qualified applicants emerged. Therefore, we believe the ideas in this chapter are useful to both women and men who want to present themselves in the best light as they look for opportunities to grow and move up in the work community. Following are first men's, then women's, perceptions of this problem area, plus efforts they are making to remedy the situations.

MEN'S PERCEPTIONS

The question we asked the men was geared to elicit ways in which they faced the problem of helping women get a fair opportunity. What we heard was most encouraging and helpful. They presented two perceptions of women's abilities and talents: One was, "I think she is talented and she knows it, too"; the other was, "I know she has the talent, but she doubts it."

For instance, Brad, an associate professor of a secondary education program at a western university wrote, "Kelly was my graduate assistant, very attractive and feminine in dress and behavior *and* very competent. She knew her job and its context as well or better than anyone in the organization. Yet others perceived her to be flighty and a typical 'dumb blonde' type. It was difficult to convince others to grant her the chance to use her skills and to receive a commensurate salary increase."

Arn, a businessman, wrote about his secretary, "Jackie was very talented, capable, dedicated, and persevering. She had all of the qualities that would make her an excellent administrator. However, her position as secretary in our company meant she was 'tracked,' and few opportunities for advancement were available."

What a benefit it would be for professional women if they all had bosses who feel as Brad and Arn do. They recognize the women's abilities but often were frustrated by their colleagues' blind-spots or organizational procedures that limit opportunities for women.

Now imagine the opposite situation where male bosses know the female subordinate or colleague is talented but she is reluctant to agree. Jerry told us, "With effort I could get Susan to recognize her capabilities, but she didn't believe enough in herself to move forward, to do something about her future."

Phil, an upper level association executive, was especially disturbed when he wrote, "Kathy won't study or prepare for added responsibility. She wants to do the minimum. She gives priority to her social life. When I try to encourage her to grab opportunities, she gives me excuses of why she can't do it."

Jim, a supervisor in the computer industry, explained in frustrated detail how his subordinate, Marna, believed that women should not be paid as well as men for equal work, nor should they seek opportunities for advancement. Although she worked full time, her home responsibilities were demanding and carried out in the most traditional way. Ordinarily the woman's choice of life style wouldn't be a problem to her employer, but Jim identified that Marna projected her values on him and the other women at work who were seeking new opportunities. No amount of talking with Marna has budged her position.

What a dilemma for these few professional men who admit that opportunities are limited for women and then who face the double barrel of resistance from their organization and peers as well as from the women themselves. What can they do?

Efforts Men Made

Coached and Counseled. Most frequently the men personally coached and counseled the women, sometimes in the form of encouraging remarks or pats on the back. Other times lengthy conversations revealed the options and barriers to advancement. One man, Jerry, described how he used an instrument listing "functional skills" to help Susan, his subordinate, see for herself what he and his colleagues recognized as her strengths. The assessment forced her to admit she had skills necessary for the project the men were preparing her to do. As Jerry said, "The instrument helped Susan to see firsthand what she wouldn't or couldn't accept from us."

Other times, the boss recognized his limitations to overcome the woman's internal barriers. Phil's solution was to facilitate Kathy's attendance at a professional workshop on career planning where he knew she might be more receptive and eventually break through her self-doubts.

Small Tests. The second method the men used was to identify and provide every opportunity for the women to take on new responsibilities, to test skills, to learn new ones, and thus to gain confidence. These opportunities for professional development came in the form of small tests and were often successful because the individual woman could face these shorter steps. The men gave the women special materials to read, invited them to attend meetings, assigned them projects they could work on together, and opened up other short-term opportunities to act independently and thus to "test the water."

Perseverance. Persistence was present in many of these men's actions, and it paid off. Arn never doubted the talents of his secretary, Jackie. He held "numerous consciousness-raising" conversations with her and gave her more responsibility. When job vacancies came up he told her about them and encouraged her to apply, even though he knew he'd eventually have to start again with a new secretary. He coached her on how to handle the interviews and it worked—she applied for and received a promotion to a middle management position.

Sometimes, the man had to take a risk and buck the traditions and practices of his organization—an arduous and time consuming task. For instance, Brad, a professor of education, took time to document Kelly's performance; he kept carbon copies of memos she had prepared and anecdotal records of daily achievements. He took this information to the chairman of his department, pointing out specific examples of her competence and how her work had helped the whole department. After much arguing, Kelly received an increase in responsibility and salary, although much smaller than her sponsor felt she deserved. However, Brad's persistence demonstrated to Kelly that her abilities were worthwhile and that others would work with her to obtain new opportunities. Unfortunately, the battle was so intense and drawn out that Kelly left for other opportunities elsewhere.

What Males Must Face

We observed two patterns in these examples. First, we were encouraged to learn about the increasing number of male bosses who recognize the talents of their women peers and subordinates. Unfortunately, these men often fought what appeared to be insurmountable odds to help the women obtain opportunities, and they often fought this battle in isolation. To us, it seems a shame the male received criticism when he should have been given organizational support and credit for making the effort to develop the abilities of a promising employee. Men who make the effort because they believe it is their responsibility as professionals, not because the law is making them do it, should be rewarded. Fortunately, the reward for this effort is the gratification of seeing one more woman utilize her talents. The organization benefits with more fully functioning employees.

The second pattern men perceived with women is the other edge of a double-edged sword. They recognize the woman's talents, and the latter responds, "Who *me*? You can't be talking about *me*!" Thus, another type of conflict may occur for the supportive male who sincerely wants to help the professional woman. He sees her talent, but his efforts to help backfire because she perceives his efforts as rescuing her and she doesn't want to be rescued. In conversations we had with several men on the role of mentors, we learned how difficult it is for them to find the fine line between appropriate mentoring behavior and inappropriate paternalistic behavior.

We believe it is unfair to professional men to always have to convince the woman she is talented. She must change her attitude from "Who *me*?" to "How nice you noticed that about me. Let's do something about it together." If the woman's self-depreciation continues, the men around her may eventually not want to be bothered. After all, why waste one's time on someone who resists encouragement? One man outlined to us innumerable efforts he made with his subordinate to get her to recognize and utilize her abilities, but in the end he fired her. He gave up. What we don't know is if he tried again with other women employees or if he was just too tired and discouraged after the first struggle.

WOMEN'S PERCEPTIONS

When women were asked, "Have you ever had a problem obtaining opportunities for advancement from your boss?" a resounding 42% said yes and 33% said it was a major problem. The examples these women shared with us revealed evidence of both blatant and subtle barriers to advancement.

Blatant Barriers

Blatant barriers are hard to overcome, but at least you know what you are up against. The following illustrations exemplify what happened when others, usually men, predetermined the limits of a woman's abilities and thus her opportunities.

You Don't Qualify. Amelia, a professional pilot, knew that in the corporate field her opportunities for positions were already narrow because of her gender. Then, once she had the job, she said, "I had to fly that much better, do everything without error, and try harder than most male pilots." She told of a time when, "a male passenger refused to fly in my plane even though he knew nothing of my credentials."

Jan, competing for a higher level position in her university, had every qualification listed on the job description, but her boss's best friend got the job. Upon investigation, she learned that the boss felt that the staff Jan would supervise wouldn't feel comfortable with a woman.

Elizabeth, a minister, told us how the bishop assigned her to a small church in the district, which meant a cut of $4,000 in her salary. He said, "You need to take this because there is nothing else available." The fact was that a male colleague of Elizabeth's who had less experience and fewer educational credentials was assigned a larger church in the same city and for a higher salary.

Hard Work Pays Off. Working hard and long hours is supposed to reap recognition and reward, at least according to the work ethic in our nation's folklore. But we learned from many women that even after "paying their dues," opportunity did not knock. A coordinator of staff development for a tri-county intermediate school district wrote, "I worked six years in my position as coordinator. I spent extra time evenings and weekends meeting the specific needs of the teachers. The evaluations of the programs I either presented or administered received excellent reviews from the participants. And yet, when a new position was announced for administrator of staff development, my boss recommended a colleague who had less experience and expertise but who was male and white."

It is difficult to be eligible for advancement when the opportunity arises, when along the way one is not recognized for accomplishments. Beverly, a woman working for a national restaurant chain, found her ideas and accomplishments continuously ignored. "It was bad enough when my well-researched idea to merge management recruitment with what I was responsible for in my role as director of personnel, was turned down, but I was surprised and hurt each time accomplishments that were smaller and of less importance were rewarded either with a promotion or increase in salary to a male achiever."

Matching Titles. Hard work may not result in a promotion, but at least if one is taking on more responsibility, a new title would be appropriate. Right? Not always. This is a "trap" many professional women keep falling into: "If I go the extra mile, do the extra project, put in extra time beyond what I'm required to do, then they'll eventually give me the promotion and new title." But, as Lynda, a secretary, told us, "Even after I did all of those things and even after my boss admitted that my job had changed, he wouldn't change my title from secretary to administrative assistant." The title was symbolic and an open admission of her status in the organization. A new title can help the individual build up new skills and use talents. But what can someone like Lynda do when she can't even get to first base with a title that matches her position on the team?

And There's More. Other blatant barriers professional women told us about included denial of attendance at professional conferences, even though male colleagues were sent. One banker was not allowed to serve on the board of the local United Way even though she had been approached from their headquarters.

Subtle Barriers

From the women's perception though, more frequently the barriers were subtle and thus much more difficult to recognize, no less to overcome.

He Is Threatened. Bev, a school consultant, was asked by another school in the same district to take over a part-time administrative role. Bev's boss's response was, "You shouldn't take the job because you are so good with students." At first glance, we might assume that the principal had the best interests of the students at heart, but Bev learned otherwise. She discovered he was threatened by her new opportunity; he would lose a competent teacher and he didn't like the inconvenience.

He Is Incompetent. Several times we heard about the frustrations of competent professionals who sensed they were dead-ended in their positions because their bosses were incompetent. In the case of Jo's boss, he made presentations of her work in a sloppy and inaccurate way, even misrepresenting her materials, thus tainting her reputation. His poor performance also reflected on others' perceptions of her. It would be difficult for her to be seen as competent by others when she was presented in this manner by her boss.

The Posted Position. Another subtle barrier to advancement, difficult to recognize but certainly unfortunate in its outcome, is the method used by many organizations when a vacancy occurs. The set-up is to pit women against each other for the same position, and the result is to jeopardize any semblance of support that may have occurred between them. Another misleading practice is to invite applications for a position when a male has been groomed or "wired" for the position. Sometimes the job description is worded to include one necessary qualification that only the male candidate is likely to have. The organization thus has appeared to have made a good faith effort, when in fact women candidates were stalled at the start.

No Invitation. Probably one of the most insidious forms of subtle barriers is being put out of the running even before the race begins. Countless women related instances in their organizations when the men would never encourage or invite women to apply for an advancement. In every case, the word used was *never*; the women were unable to think of an occasion when either they or another woman was sought out or encouraged. It was as if women did not exist.

On the other hand, the flip side of this subtle barrier is that the women were waiting to be asked. One can wait a long time before opportunity might knock at one's particular door. But we also heard the yearning in many women, "If I just work hard enough, get enough education, do the extra, they might notice me." This waiting game rarely paid off for the women involved. It was often this trait that frustrated the supportive males we wrote about earlier in this chapter: "What are they waiting for? Don't they see the opportunity in front of their noses?" And why should women expect others to notice them, to ask them to apply for a promotion?

Efforts Made by Women

When faced with both the overt and the subtle barriers, what did these women do?

Nothing. Sometimes they literally did nothing. They waited. Some fumed as they watched others get the opportunity, begrudgingly giving support to the man who got the job. Sometimes they just could not overcome whatever was in them that wouldn't allow them to fight for opportunity for themselves. Beverly, who works in the restaurant business, recognized in herself "an inability to fight for me; often it is so much easier for me to 'go to the wall' for a subordinate than for myself."

Prepared Self. Sometimes the waiting period was used to develop areas needing special attention. Many went to workshops and even back to school to pick up skills they lacked. They knew that the next time they would be ready with the right set of qualifications. Male and female professionals frequently mentioned three essential areas: negotiating, diagnosing, and presenting skills. When one woman protested, "I just don't know how to negotiate," her male colleague warned, "Then if you don't know how to negotiate and sell what you have to offer, someone else will and you'll be no farther ahead."

The second essential skill mentioned throughout our interviews was learning how to assess oneself and one's organization. Diagnosing personal and organizational strengths and weaknesses preceded the development of a plan of action.

The third essential skill mentioned was learning how to present one's ideas in a manner that others would understand and that would reflect positively on the presenter. Jo, whose boss presented her material so poorly, found success when she learned to prepare the material differently. "I wrote a brief summary, highlighting in yellow pen the significant points, and then I briefed him verbally. I gave copies of the materials to pertinent staff members. I attended the meeting so that all questions could be answered properly." As Jo's boss looked better, so did she.

Gathered Forces. Many of the women rallied together with others who were interested in opening up opportunities for women. Elizabeth, the minister, formed a network of other women clergy to share perceptions of the problem, exchange information, and develop strategies. Supportive male clergy became members of this informal network. It worked. Recently a woman was appointed pastor to a large, prestigious urban church.

A second form of gathering forces was to develop a mentor relationship with someone who was supportive and yet influential enough to assist in seeking and obtaining opportunities.

Closely Watched-and-Prepared Strategy. Many women became more alert. They learned how vacancies were advertised and made sure they were informed of them. They ferreted out hard-to-find information, and when an opportunity emerged, they were ready with current and vital supportive materials to present their qualifications.

Specifics on how a person can organize information about oneself and present it in the best possible light were given by a man who had both applied for many jobs and hired many employees. He said, "Since competition is keen for positions, outline your skills in the order and manner that you know will be most needed for the position. Of course, this means you incorporate what you have learned about the position and the particular organization during your investigation. Be sure to include, in writing or verbally, personal characteristics you know would also enhance your ability to handle the new position."

Persistent Communication. Persistence and communication worked hand in hand for many women. They knew they wanted something, and they didn't give up. They used every chance they could to plead their cases with their bosses. Lynda, the secretary who wanted a new title, kept explaining to her boss why she needed and deserved the title. Even when he tried the diversionary tactic of asking her to research how other companies handled it, she didn't get discouraged. She used this as her foot in the door, did the research, and got the title.

Amelia, the pilot, says she "continues to do my absolute best and exhibit professionalism in my flying at all times. Even though it's hard, I aim for perfection in all things as I hold on to the belief that my abilities will be recognized by those who count."

In one group interview several of our colleagues agreed that probably the wisest thing they have observed was when the individual communicated specific needs for professional growth at the time of starting a new job and periodically thereafter. They felt that it benefited both the employee and the employer when the subject of opportunities for advancement and for professional growth as well as the subject of the benefits package were discussed at the interview and during the orientation period. They said, "It's up to the employee to initiate and continue this communication as long as the need exists."

An applicant for the directorship of a YMCA developed a two-part proposal outlining her plans for the first year and subsequent needs for future years. It included a realistic presentation of problems and suggestions on how to overcome them. Her plan for professional advancement was specific, realistic, and long-term, and she got the job!

A New Position. Some women did a thorough assessment of personal skills and the needs of the organization and then used the information to propose a new position. It took careful planning and a persuasive presentation to those who would make the final decision.

Created Publicity. More than one person kept a personal file on her ideas and suggestions and copies of her exemplary work. She used them whenever the opportunity arose to let others know about her ideas. Some people sent them "up the pipeline," properly credited. Many women found they built a reputation as a competent person this way and used the information when applying for a new position.

Quit. Some women dropped out mentally as demonstrated in Chapter 2 on motivation. What a loss to both the employee and employer to have mental dropouts in either delivery of services or productivity. Others, like Kelly, admitted that their present situation was incompatible with their individual abilities and needs and sought opportunities else-where. This was often not an avoidance, but rather a well-thought-out option. Those who used what they had previously learned when applying for the next position had a stronger negotiating position.

What is sad about this is that the employer lost someone who could have been an important contributor. He'll have to start again with a search, then with orientation and training. Most likely he'll never try to under-stand why the woman left and what it was about the organizational policies and procedures that exacerbated the situation.

Equally unfortunate, though, is the myth held by the woman who quit that "somewhere out there, someone will give me a chance to use my talents." Her "Alice in Wonderland" journey may be fruitless; she probably will find herself again in similar work surroundings. Perhaps the barriers will come in a different form, but most likely they'll still exist. We believe the cycle will be broken when more employees, both male and female, become sensitive to these barriers for advancement. The sheer number of these people will force changes in the organizational norms and attitudes. For women, finding a supportive boss helps, but if he is alone in his battle, both could experience a battle not unlike Don Quixote's and Sanchez's frustrating fight with the windmill.

Opportunity is knocking . . . perhaps not as loudly for women . . . but astute listeners will hear it and respond. Success may not come as quickly as wished or in the form hoped for, but *it is possible.*

13

YOU'RE
AT WORK NOW

It's Monday A.M., with the usual rush to get prepared for another work week, not only physically prepared but mentally making the transition from the weekend pace. After a few hours of adjustment the work's momentum increases; tasks listed for this week are checked off. But look! On the list is an item that doesn't seem to belong: Call the dentist to check on daughter's X-rays. So between other business calls, the dentist is called, perhaps surreptitiously.

What appears as an inconsequential event is actually significant in the lives of countless men and women. Daily they experience problems when they try to resolve the dilemma of separating one's personal life from one's paid work life. Who is experiencing these problems at work? In what form do individuals face these circumstances? What do bosses and employers have to say about them? What about the impact on other family members? Are the results all negative or are trends to help employees find productive solutions emerging?

WHOSE PROBLEM IS IT?

Both the men and women we surveyed are experiencing this problem of separating work and personal lives. Forty-two percent of the women answered yes to the question, "Have you ever had a problem separating your work from your home responsibilities or solving practical problems such as child care, demands for overtime, or requests for flex-time?" One-fifth of them said it was a major problem.

We made the assumption, and correctly so, that men's part in this dilemma would be different, so we asked them, "Have you ever had the problem of determining how to keep her (the female peer, boss, or subordinate) personal life separate from work and to what degree your organization should provide answers to practical problems such as child care and flex-time?" Twenty-six percent of the men said yes, and 13% said it represented a major problem.

Traditionally women have found their cultural place based in the home and family, whereas men's place has centered outside the home. Therefore, we believe the dilemma in this issue of separating work and home is different for working women, who are going against tradition. For women the dilemma is justifying the new extension from home to work; for men it is justifying the extension from work to home.

In a study of 307 middle-class women in Evanston, Illinois, sociologist Catherine White Berheide reported that these women had the same experiences as those reported by the working women we surveyed: Women do the majority of all housework. Berheide's research revealed women did 80% to 90% of the housework in their homes. And this work involved eighty different activities. The full-time homemaker was found to work eight hours a day, seven days a week. Women with part-time jobs worked seven hours a day at managing the household, and the full-time worker spent another five hours a day working at home. It is amazing that women have any time to sleep at all.

When Berheide explored how these hours changed when the woman had children, she discovered that it wasn't the number of children but the simple fact of having children that increased the workload. Both working and nonworking mothers indicated they spent about 53% of their household working time on activities revolving around children. As a result the women with children worked an average of 7.5 hours daily doing housework; women without children, 5.5 hours.[1]

Berheide's research showed that men at home tended to engage in two household tasks more often than women: handling the family accounts and doing repairs. Another research group recently found that when both husband and wife shared household responsibilities, the men shopped 32% of the time and cooked 47%; 80% claimed they took care of the children.[2]

So if working women have these additional hours of personal responsibilities to fit into the week, when do they do it? Contrary to men who tend to do their household chores on evenings and weekends, most working women rise earlier, work through every evening and weekend, and *bring the added burden to their workplace.* So it seems to be the fact that women who work simply neither have enough assistance from family members nor enough hours in the day, that causes this problem of keeping their personal lives out of the workday.

However, to set the record straight, it wasn't only women who expressed concern about this problem as a personal dilemma. Men told us of personal demands on their time that often could not wait to be resolved after work hours. This trend is not surprising when you look at the statistics that reveal increasing numbers of divorced or remarried men who have full- or part-time custody of their children. Added to this are increasing numbers of men who are articulating their sincere interest in their families and who, as a result, are requesting more flexible work time to maintain and enrich family life.

The preceding may give the impression that only women and men with family responsibilities experience the problem of separating their personal life from work. Single women also carry over personal errands, social problems, and domestic responsibilities into work time. This may appear surprising considering that as single people without family members making daily demands they should have more free time to accomplish these tasks. However, we observe that it is women in general who either have not learned or perhaps accepted the division between personal and work life—it is not one's marital status. Men have internalized the concept of separation of work and personal life. Women have not.

The business organization traditionally is not prepared for employ-

[1]Dustin Harvey, United Press International, *The Billings Gazette,* Billings, Mont., August 14, 1980.

[2]Benton & Bowles, Inc., *Boardroom Reports,* December 29, 1980.

ees with these new demands and extra burdens. The norm for defining one's role at work was created by the millions of working men who had women in their lives who assumed the burden of their husbands' personal life responsibilities. We found in our survey that many employers are still greatly perplexed concerning what to do with these working women and changing men.

WHO SHOULD RESOLVE THE PROBLEM?

Whose problem is it to resolve—the individual, the family, or the organization? Let's look at the following cases to gain three different perspectives on the dilemma of separating one's work from one's personal life.

It's My Problem. Susan, aged forty, returned to work for only three days a week after fifteen years as a full-time homemaker. Her words represented what we frequently heard from women. "Learning to separate my work from my personal life is *not* a problem I have with the men at work—it is *my own* problem," said Susan. As she told us more about this, Susan admitted she might be assuming this dilemma as her problem because for the past fifteen years her primary responsibility was to ensure a continuously smooth-running family life. To resolve the extra demands on her because of job and home, she organizes herself and her family. This is a common solution women choose—they become an even more efficient, but still, overall manager of the home. Through careful planning and increased involvement of family members in household chores, Susan manages to avoid the spill-over into her work life, thus she perceives no conflict with the men at work.

On the surface it appears there is no conflict. However, to assume such responsibility means that Susan has assumed she is truly expected to, and is capable of doing it *all*. She has swallowed the myth that women are endlessly expandable. If Susan takes a full-time working position and continues to manage and/or do most of the home and child care, she will find herself testing the "superwoman" standard. When she can't live up to or do all these activities (and who can?), she may feel that she has failed as a person.

From what we learned of Susan's circumstances, her family was more cooperative than most; at least they agreed to do the tasks she outlined on her home management plan. But if her work hours increase, if family members become less cooperative, or if she were a single parent, the men at the workplace may well begin to notice how much more often she brings personal tasks to her workday.

What About Us? The employee is pulled in and from many directions. The needs of others in our personal lives are varied and often urgent; these needs do not go away just because we are at work.

Darlene, single and a middle manager in hospital administration, found that when her father was hospitalized her boss put extra pressure on her by making snide remarks. He would say, "I'll give you the luxury of not docking your pay even though you have spent long lunch hours visiting your father."

Paul, a social worker, had total sympathy and cooperation from his employers when his wife was terminally ill. They encouraged him to take time off to visit her and to maintain the extra parental duties required at this time of crisis. Paul said what made this extraordinary was that his superiors were generally perceived as authoritarian and distant.

Elizabeth, a social worker in another agency, when hearing Paul describe what had happened to him, said that when she wants to attend her child's play at school she gets resistance. Together we were all speculating if Paul's employers were cooperative because his was a crisis situation rather than a normal, everyday request or if the responses depended on who asked for the time off—the male or the female.

A single parent of three teenage children, Nancy enjoys her job as an accountant. Conflict arises when she needs to work extra hours in the evening or on weekends and her children have activities which she also wants to attend. She especially feels the pinch when one of her children is ill. She weighs the importance of her job against her home responsibilities and generally chooses her family. She must be striking a correct balance because she claims her male boss and colleagues do not criticize her decisions.

John, in partnership with his wife as therapists, indicates that the difficulty of separating work from the personal sphere is because it is convenient to carry over the extra work into one's personal time. Although their professional work is meaningful, this couple values time to relax and to enjoy their personal relationship. Through frequent reviews of each of their needs, they schedule their lives so each part is included, thus they said they experience a high degree of success.

"But we're not paying you to take care of your personal life." At work the boss and often colleagues were disturbed when personal responsibilities spilled over—"after all, you're here to work," they would say. A dramatic shift in responses emerged in our research. All of the following examples represent the traditional notion of the proper behaviors for employees while on "company time."

Sam, a married man, watched with empathy as his colleague, Andrea, struggled to keep up with her work as a computer programmer in a fast-growing firm and to still find time to manage her family. He noted that it was particularly hard for Andrea because she did not want to have children in the first place. Conceding to her husband's wishes for children, she was now torn between the daily demands of the job and the extra duties she must perform at home. Sam watched as Andrea would sneak in calls to her babysitter or doctor, because when the calls were openly made, her colleagues made snide comments, such as "You sure make a lot of personal calls."

Many bosses told us of instances when female subordinates took excessive time off from work to meet family demands or spent excessive time during working hours talking on the phone on personal matters. Ron, a top executive in the government, was continually irritated by Rita's behavior. Although she was living with her spouse, she carried the weight of home demands. Ron observed that Rita seemed constantly wrapped up in emergencies and arrangements for her two children. During one period Ron even kept track of the amount of time involved. He chose an indirect method of resolution, which met with low success. His casual comments never penetrated or were ignored, and Rita still makes her calls.

Other men handle this dilemma through rigid and direct enforcement of rules. One radio producer informed his employee that all of her personal errands and tasks must be done during her break or at lunchtime. "Not much success," he said ruefully, "maybe a rating of two on a scale of one to five," with five the highest degree of success.

A middle school principal, also a wife and mother, when observing that the working mothers who taught in her school rarely made themselves available for after-school student assistance, discussed the problem with the union representative and key teachers. Her position, although sympathetic, was unbending: It was unfair to the students and to those teachers who put in the extra time. She reported a rating of one—the lowest degree of success.

No wonder! Those who firmly believe that the employee should leave personal life at the door of the office and who try to solve the recurring problem through reinforcement of policy or standards or insisted on only one behavior only exacerbated the problem. The problems themselves did not go away.

SO WHAT CAN YOU DO?

As the solutions we discussed in other chapters, the solution to the issue at hand crystallized at three levels: the individual, boss-employee, and organizational. Similar to the other conflicts at work, solutions start with personal awareness and involve tremendous commitment and cooperation.

One intelligent solution suggested by one professional was preventative medicine: Clarify one's expectations during the job-selection process. Rather than wait until after you are on the job, our professionals agreed that it was important to explain to a prospective employer what personal demands might arise to interfere with one's workday.

Sylvia, director of a community agency, told us that during a job interview Jane assertively stated, "On Fridays, I teach the blind from 2:00 until 5:00 P.M." Sylvia was so impressed with Jane's commitment and assuredness that she cooperated. Sylvia's decision paid off because Jane demonstrated that her work would not suffer. She made up any lost time and work without fanfare. In fact, it was this quality in many of the professionals we interviewed that seemed to make the difference. Those that automatically arranged to make up any lost time found they received less criticism from peers and bosses.

But what if the employer is not so supportive? We were told the employee has three choices: (1) Do it anyway. Take the risk; go ahead and attend your child's play. Be sure to make up the work and perhaps, with time, others will be more accepting. (2) Challenge the resistance. Ask, "Do you have any questions about my work, its quality, and promptness? Then there is no problem if I take two hours to go to my son's school?" We quickly recognized that this position requires confidence in one's self and abilities. (3) The third choice is to work with the boss. Many were quite willing to discuss the conflict, look for options, and take the risk of establishing a new work norm.

Sometimes the total acceptance of the agreement between boss and employee didn't come immediately. In Margaret's case the solution was not complete, but her boss did grant her flexible time—a legitimate option in that particular government agency. He still complains to others that Margaret's utilization of the flex-time plan takes advantage of him. By the tone of his complaint it is clear that he is more disturbed by the "inconvenience" to him than any shirking of work on Margaret's part.

Contrasted with Margaret's situation is Karen's success. Her boss valued her and her work enough not only to circumvent the system in which they worked and to provide her with flexible working hours, but he defended her and their arrangement. When he heard negative comments about Karen's schedule, he either ignored the remarks or responded head-on. As a result, Karen is highly motivated, completes all of her projects promptly, and deeply respects her boss.

Fortunately, bosses who want to find creative solutions to this dilemma do not always have to buck the system. New organizational policies and procedures help employees find a sense of balance and quality in their lives. We are especially amazed when large institutions such as the federal government and large companies, Hewlitt-Packard, for one, lead the way by encouraging their employees to participate in community activities.

Even churches, often the bastions of rigidity, are changing. The United Methodist Church, aware that job transfers can play havoc with family life, are meeting the challenge. Some bishops who, in the course of their duties determine placement of ministers in their area churches, are now weighing the impact of the proposed transfer on the male or female minister who has a working spouse and/or children.

Recognition by institutions and business that men and women who work also have personal lives gives us hope that our original question is finally being addressed. Originally our research question elicited responses that endorsed the norm that one's work and personal life *should* be separated. But our position is that work and personal demands *cannot* be separated and that attempts to do so perpetuate the problem, leading to frustrated and tired employees.

Individual employees and decision-makers in organizations need to be committed to the belief that an integration of work, recreational, family, spiritual, emotional, aesthetic, and intellectual needs within our daily lives leads to a more meaningful and productive existence at work and at home.

With this commitment as the foundation, alternative ways of integrating the needs of work and home can be explored, tried, and evaluated. Without the commitment and collaborative problem-solving working hand in hand, the attitude—"Leave your personal life at the office door, you're at work now"—will continue.

14

BLUEPRINT
FOR REACHING
ACROSS DIFFERENCES

We began this book with a purpose. We wanted to explore territory that had been avoided for too long. We knew, because we are woman and man, that when women and men seek to relate together for a given period of time, their differences will become an important factor in their survival together. We also felt the work setting was a prime area for our exploration. Women and men struggle side by side for monetary gain. What we found was what we suspected. Women and men are having trouble coexisting in coherent and trusting work relationships. They are merely surviving side by side.

Our purpose, then, was to ask whether women and men face similar problems in the work setting, and, if so, what they are doing about these problems. Our hope was to discover the dynamics that permeate and undergird the male-female work dilemma and then to offer some solutions, or hope. The road to discovery has been one of polarities, one of simplicity and complexity. We found that, in general, men behave certain ways in all walks of life and that they do not question their behavior. Women likewise accept "their place" as "that's the way it is supposed to be." It is both very simple and very complex at the same time.

THE PROBLEMS ARE NOT
ALL MALE OR ALL FEMALE

In most cases of marital synchronization, it is a known fact that it takes two people to make a successful marriage and it can take two to cause its demise. One party may be more guilty than the other, but both persons contribute to the harmony or disharmony of the union. So it is in the work scene. It has been easy, because of present literature and our own research, to make men the culprits. The problems seem to rest on male dominance and ignorance. We admit to our struggle in seeking a sense of equality concerning "who owns the problem of work dissatisfaction." We believe the problems created at work are not simply caused just by males or just by females, but that they result from the "negative energy" that seems to flow among boss, peer, or subordinate, be they male or female.

Ideally we have tried to individualize the concerns men and women have with one another and among themselves as they work together. Sometimes a person is disgruntled or uneasy, not because he or she is male or female, but because of the situation. It might not have a thing to do with one's gender. That is the ideal. Realistically, though, most persons respond to other individuals out of their femaleness or maleness, thus making it a gender problem. And when gender gets mixed up in the situations, the problem also becomes one of equality. When equality enters the picture, men and women alike fight for their rights. The fight for rights is both a male problem and a female problem.

WHAT WE FOUND

Being researchers and writers with educational, theological, and psychological orientations, we naturally looked for certain aspects of how men and women related to one another in the work setting. A scientist or mathematician might draw some of the same conclusions as we did, but with a different emphasis.

The Root of the Problem

Foremost, we found the problems created in the work scene were, first of all, gender oriented; second, boss, subordinate, and peer oriented; and third, self-imposed ("I don't deserve any better; I must accept who and where I am in my life."). We are hopeful that a new awareness came to some of the persons who completed our questionnaire and attended our research groups. Many began with the premise of simply accepting one's lot at work and feeling futile about the possibility of any change taking place. Their reasons were not always easily identifiable as being gender oriented, since the roots of the problems were unexposed. Once the histories began to be uncovered, understandings emerged, and new strategies looked possible.

The Intensity of the Problem

We found men and women perceived the work problems with a different intensity. This is not surprising given women's history in the job market. They are infants in their new style of decision-making and in believing that they can hold positions of power in a male-dominated world of work. The woman's struggle for acceptance, which grows out of a state of work oppression, would naturally elevate her need to express extreme feelings concerning her longing for equality with males.

With the exception of two categories on our questionnaire—sexual attractiveness and fewer privileges—women stated they had experienced problems at work in the other ten categories more frequently than men. The greatest discrepancy was in the area of authority. Sixty-five percent of the women questioned stated that their lack of equal recognition in the work force was a major problem. They did not feel their ideas mattered or were considered as valid as those presented by men. In other words, the "punch of authority" was missing where women were concerned. A meager .03% of the men perceived authority as a problem. This discrepancy is revealing and certainly points to the difference of intensity between women and men as each perceives the work problem.

Other statistics can be reviewed in Tables 1-1 and 1-2 in the first chapter. As inferred and specifically mentioned in the foregoing pages of this book, men, who have been in charge of the work scenes for years, would have a more difficult time getting in touch with the issues as being deep problems. Women, who have felt victimized, understandably perceive most of the issues more extremely.

The Gaps in Perception of Problems

We found certain gaps to be the key reasons for the differences in the intensity of the twelve problems. For instance, there is a gap in the basic understanding of a man's and a woman's approach to life, which carries over into their work. Men seem to be more *goal oriented*, whereas women are more *role oriented*. Stated another way, men are schooled in the ways of winning and achieving, sometimes at all costs. Women seek meaning to the questions, "Who am I?" "What am I?" and "Where do I go from here?" Parenthetically, it is interesting to note what happens to a woman who discovers her competitive side and to a man who begins asking the questions of ultimate meaning for his life. When this happens there is a narrowing of the gaps. The problem is that in many individuals not enough questioning is taking place; thus, the male and female preoccupation with goals and roles, respectively, continues, and the gap persists.

Another distancing was found in a man's and a woman's interpretation of power. Men seem to want to hold on to power. Women seek to share power. Men do not want to lose what has been granted to them through history, be it right or wrong; women want to experience some of this power. The struggle for equal rights gets lost in the fear that if men relinquish some of their power, women will not know what to do with it; and if a woman is granted power, she might not be trusted with it. So, the gap widens. As one woman said of another, "We do not need a woman mayor in this town. Women are just not cut out to be in a position to represent this big city. Men are the decision-makers, and that is just the way it ought to be."

Even women wonder what to do with the power once it comes their way. So men continue to hold onto the positions of strength in this present-day society, knowing they will most likely remain the power brokers. Certainly such a mentality can only enhance the gap of equality and foster further frustration among the seekers of new power.

Another gap, and closely related to the prior one, is the need for men to have control over others at all levels in business settings, versus the desire for women to seek control over themselves and a measure of control over others. It borders upon degrees but is manifested in action. It is suffocating to be around a person who demands that you respond to your work tasks the way he or she wants you to respond, rather than how your talents and imagination fit into the scheme of things. A boss of such insensitivity awakens in the employee the need for some control over his or her own life. The employee is suddenly confronted with the question, "Is this job worth dying for?"

It is difficult for the man to let loose of the control factor. It is also difficult for the woman to know how much control she deserves over another person in the work setting. A woman has no difficulty answering the question of control in her traditional role of homemaker; but she struggles for a compromise to this issue of control at work. She certainly wants to survive and it is the *quality* of her survival that causes the gap. It is almost as if she is saying, "What kind of control and how much do I really deserve?" It is a question the slaves asked themselves at their emancipation; it was almost comfortable having someone else in control.

The fourth gap we discerned was the difference between men and women in wanting to discuss the issues. Men, even though they did enter into many hours of dialogue with us, often gave the impression there wasn't much to talk about. This outlook is understandable. When the world of work is going in your favor, why rock the boat? Another way of stating it is: Men had a more difficult time picking out the issues and then wading through them. Women, on the other hand, felt there was much to talk about. This, too, is quite understandable. They wanted not only to rock the present work boat, but to consider the possibility of building a new one! In a real sense this book is a mini-blueprint for a new working structure. It is a desire to take both extremes—"We (males) don't have much to talk about" and "We (females) have much to say and we want to be heard"—and blending them into a productive new beginning. As the gap narrows, the dialogue increases and a new appreciation of one another as men and women is born.

The Awareness that Change Is Possible

We also found persons from all walks of work, backgrounds, and perceptions stimulated by the possibility of a new awakening. We are not speaking about a glorious new birth for all working men and women in which they acknowledge their past and develop a new equality at work. We are rather suggesting that persons seemed willing to grapple with their new found awareness, even though such an awareness had the ingredients of defensiveness, pain, and incongruity.

Willingness to Enter into Dialogue

Willingness to be in dialogue with one another, or to respond on a piece of paper (questionnaire) was clearly expressed by both men and women. The dialogue often took the form of a monologue, but ideas and feelings were aired and new directions discussed. We found that the various concerns we proposed to females and males did not always find agreement. Our goal was not that persons agree with one another, but rather that they understand where others were coming from. Simply stated, the goal for our dialogue with participants was clarification of issues, not agreement. If clarity could be reached, it would provide a breeding ground for understanding. Out of understanding would come new possibilities. We were elated to discover persons giving themselves to this process of evolution, from clarity to newness.

WE HOPE IN HOPE

There have been times when the research for this book seemed mired in the bog of "status quo." The Biblical cry of "show me a sign" seemed to be the heartfelt plea of the various persons who so graciously gave themselves to this project. And signs of hope did emerge through the months of research. Although no one conclusion can be drawn to indicate that a particular course is the proper or right direction, a variety of options did appear on the horizon of work equality. Here are eight possibilities imprinted with the footsteps of hope.

1. Hope in New Awareness. We began with the "pinch"—the twinges of discomfort all of us experience in our lives from time to time. Pinches can move us to self-assessment or a new awareness of ourselves. When we are willing to shout "ouch," then we are also ready to examine the source of the hurt. Our concern is that we do not wait too long and then find that we missed the key opportunity to effect some change in ourselves and in others.

When Bruce was struggling with a decision, he told Todd, his counselor, "I think I will just dwell on this for a while. When the time is right I will make a decision as to what to do."

Todd looked at Bruce intently and said, "How much time do you have?"

"What do you mean?" asked Bruce.

"I don't know what I mean, except how much time do you have, Bruce?" was the counselor's reply.

The question is also relevant to the individual discovering a new awareness or idea that needs acting out. To offer the possibility of change in the work force by engaging oneself in any one of the twelve areas offered in this book is also to answer the question, "How much time do I have?" *Time is short.*

The time may be now. Ouch!

2. Hope in a New Conspiracy. It is subtle, but most men would not be in a questing place if women were not seeking some order around their identity. Men are "spinning off" women's searchings. Past states of contentment are being challenged and reordered. When men catch the fire of the new ideas of work equalization and honestly put them into action, then both men and women will find themselves part of what Marilyn Ferguson calls the new conspiracy.

Ms. Ferguson, in her research for the book, *The Aquarian Conspiracy,* notes that several men she questioned felt the women's movement was important for their own change, "not only because it focused on the trampled potentials of half the human race but also because it questioned the supremacy of those masculine characteristics valued in the society: competition, manipulation, aggression, objectivity." She continues, "As women in transformation are discovering their sense of self and vocation, men are discovering the reward of sensitive relationships. During these equalizing shifts, the basis for male-female interaction is being redefined. Men are becoming more feeling and intuitive; women, more autonomous and purposeful."[1] There is hope in this form of change. To be a conspirator is to listen, evaluate, and act, not out of old roles, but rather with a sense of newness.

3. Hope in Humor. The old saying, "It is easier to laugh than to cry," may be quite applicable for those struggling for a new definition of work equality. New behavior takes courage and can have its moments of stumbling. To exhibit constant criticism toward either a man or woman

[1]Marilyn Ferguson, *The Aquarian Conspiracy*, (Los Angeles: J.P. Tarcher, Inc., 1980), p. 389.

may build barriers and mount up tension. Female-male issues need to be addressed with astute listening and recognition of trial and error as part of the new process. Humor can be a catalyst to adventure.

4. Hope in Learning Problem-Solving Methods. As mentioned earlier, most of us are very eager to point out problems, but not as quick to propose ways to solve the discomforts. Problem-solving techniques might well find themselves tacked to office walls and company bulletin boards. Boss, peer, and subordinate all need skills to help realize new directions out of the maze of problems that hinder production and self-actualization.

Most problem-solving methods are not that difficult. Outlined below is one method that all levels of employment can utilize.

a. Identify the issue. Something is missing; a tension needs relief; there is a gap between things as they are and things as I want them.
b. Identify who is causing the problem. What is *my* contribution to the problem? What is my *boss's* contribution, my peer's, or my subordinate's? Is the problem an organizational one?
c. Identify who is being affected by the problem. Is this just my problem or is the whole organization suffering?
d. Brainstorm possible solutions to the problem. Without deep thought or evaluation, enumerate as many ideas as possible. For example, "We need a seminar on 'role awareness' for this company."
e. Select three courses of action and evaluate them, choosing the one most likely to meet the problem head on. All ideas should be considered, but hopefully two or three will appear above the rest as the best alternatives to move the organization or individual toward a solution.
f. Identify a strategy for carrying out the action. This will involve who, when, where, and how.
g. Test the solution; experiment with actual involvement. It is one thing to identify the problem, the culprit, and the new direction to take. The most difficult decision is the one to *act*.
h. Evaluate the results. Searching for new ways to bring about a sense of fairness and equality in the work setting may need revision over and over again. Evaluating how attitudes and actions have changed is vitally important to further action.

    i. Incorporate new information. The learning process allows new ideas and energies to emerge. By continually adding these new learnings and experiences, new strategies for attacking the problem will develop naturally.

    j. Act again. A jewel is not brought to perfect refinement until it has been polished again and again. Individuals and organizations will not know the beauty of creative conflict and resolution until many processes have been experienced. Remember, we are dealing with years of cultural history.

    k. Continue to evaluate and act again.

    5. Hope in Educational Opportunities. We are all teachers, one to another. Specific seminars might be offered on work equality, but the deep hope for learning lies in each of us being a mentor to a co-worker. The churches call it witnessing. We call it being an educational opportunist. Simply stated, take every opportunity to teach someone else. We are all a compilation of our experiences. We are what we have seen, heard, smelled, tasted, touched, and loved combined into one neat package called you or me. It is a learning evolution. There is hope men and women will continue to be teachers. The classroom is anywhere you find yourself in dialogue with another seeker. The material you present is your expression of a better way for women and men to work side by side, to each feel a sense of power, to each be unwilling to misuse it.

    6. Hope in the Networking Process. We do not live in isolation. Most human beings want a support system they can count on. To feel alone is to be unaware of those persons "out there" who also desire a sense of equality. Groups that band together for a cause find strength in the journey. It is called networking. If you feel unsupported in your tasks for acting out a new strategy for work survival, we suggest you find those co-workers among you—or others outside the work setting—who are experiencing some of the same turmoil and form a network of support. Within such a group, new ideas for action, and hopefully for change, may emerge.

    7. Hope in Role Reversal. One of our research groups began with these instructions: "We want each of you to take on a separate identity for thirty minutes. Men, you are to decide what kind of a woman you would like to be, how you would look, your likes and dislikes, your dreams, your causes, your vocation, and anything that feeds your womanhood.

Women, you are to do the same, only become a man. Choose the kind of man you wish to be. After each of you have taken on this new identity, we want you to tell us your new name and who you are. Please speak in the first person."

The new people emerged with a new sense of awareness. Each presented themselves with a sense of "is this what it is really like? Would this actually be me?" One man struggled for words to describe his "womanness." At the end of his new revelation he said, "I'm feeling very sad. I have always wanted to know what it is like to have a baby so that part of me is fulfilled. But as I tell you more about my life as a woman, especially in this society, I am hurting. I wonder if there is really any hope for me? I am a protester of living as an unequal among insensitive people who don't seem to care. I am reaching out for something to hold onto, but it keeps eluding me because I'm not sure I can trust my world to be different. I feel angry and hurt. It is hard for me to talk about it."

When that kind of intensity enters each of our minds and emotions, then there will be hope. We may have to switch the roles in our fantasies for a brief time to recognize the agony. But, once recognized, men and women can become a part of one another's solutions.

8. Hope in Little Miracles. We would be amiss to believe huge changes will occur all at once and that attitudes and behaviors will quickly reverse themselves. Our utopian dream is a society with completely equal working relationships. Realistically, we have been a long time formulating the patterns of our culture that have us in the questing place today. Changes will not happen overnight. However, if corporate structures humanize the individuals that give that structure its identity, and if men and women give credence to each other's journeys toward a new equality, a small, but very important step will have been taken. One attitude change by a boss, peer, or subordinate that improves working conditions may not statistically shatter the world, but a small improvement is better than no improvement. Immobility and stagnation are cancers to the vitality of organizational effectiveness.

A FINAL WORD

When noted anthropologist Margaret Mead was asked what one idea she would insist be taught a person today, she said people should learn to feel deeply what it means to deal with the concept of change. Change is the key.

Our book will have served its purpose, if, to some degree, we have helped you understand your past, evaluate your present, and find stimulus for a changing future. By facing the realities of today's changing work roles you will spare yourself the trauma of continual misunderstanding and criticism. New awareness can empower women and men, together and separately, to enrich one another in working relationships. It is time to recognize that people are not obstacles to avoid or jump over. Women and men are people of freedom who have the capacity to believe as never before that in all of life, especially in the world of work, it is possible to meaningfully reach across differences.

APPENDICES

THE QUESTIONNAIRE

A difficult problem facing us as writers-researchers was the methodology we would use to gather our information. To assist us in making our decision, we reviewed educational research methods we had previously used in our graduate work and methods currently used in other sociological studies and books. We analyzed the benefits, costs, and our capability of conducting a statistically reliable research project.

We concluded that the purpose of our study was to encourage dialogue between working men and women, not to conduct pure research and thus publish the results to a limited audience. If we had attempted to do pure research, we realized it probably would not be done by us, because we were both limited in resources and time. Also, we were determined to get the dialogue going as soon as possible. Purely quantitative results would bog down the proposed timetable.

Thus, we decided to conduct a study based on our knowledge of research methods, but with a limited sample. We would not attempt to generalize from our data to "every working man or woman," but to use the information as a springboard for further discussion and exploration.

How would we reach the professionals who could give us the information? With a large population, limited time, and money, we chose to use survey research as the predominant method to gather preliminary information.

With the assistance of a professional researcher, Kathleen McAngus of Denver, we went through the difficult process of selecting the topics to be studied. Based on our knowledge of current literature and from our own professional experiences, we listed, refined, and pretested categories of conflict between women and men. After several revisions, we settled on the twelve categories as seen in the following questionnaires.

The process of refining the questions in each category was difficult. To gather the information we wanted, it was necessary to phrase the questions differently, depending on whether the questionnaire was answered by a man or a woman. Thus, the form of the questions differed in all categories except etiquette, the first category, and sexual attractiveness, the fifth category.

The questionnaire consisted of a cover letter and six parts. Part I established who each respondent should be thinking about as the questions were answered. We knew it would be easier if they could think about specific individuals of the opposite gender rather than all the men or all the women with whom they had dealt. We limited their focus to relationships they had had within the past two years. We were interested in problems that occurred with specific persons and that person's role: boss, peer-colleague, or subordinate.

The purpose of Part II was to quickly analyze what had caused the most problems for them. With the three persons in mind that they earlier had identified, the respondents were asked to answer twelve questions with either a "yes" or "no" and to designate with whom they had experienced the problems.

Part III listed the twelve categories and allowed the respondent to rate the seriousness of each conflict area. This step narrowed the focus of the respondent in preparation for Part IV.

Since our study's purpose was to present both the problems experienced by men and women (for comparison purposes), and to identify solutions attempted by these professionals, Part IV was crucial in our exploration. We asked them to elaborate on any three of the problem areas, preferably the three that gave them the greatest concern or represented their greatest success. We promised the respondents anonymity, thus when we used this information in the text, their names and titles were changed, but not the content of their responses.

Part V gave us background demographic information that clarified details about the problems and attempts at resolution.

Part VI was necessary in the event we wanted further information or additional persons to contact.

The questionnaire served as the basis for our survey research in contacting our sample by mail and in direct contact through interviews and workshops.

APPENDIX I:
MEN'S VERSION

Leadership △ Dynamics

Dr. Lois B. Hart • (303) 823-5146   Box 320 • Lyons, Co. 80540

August 29, 198X

Dear Colleague:

We have selected you to participate in an important research study. We are trying to determine the extent of professional and personal conflict between men and women within the work environment, which we know exists based on our experience and current literature. Our main purpose is to identify strategies to overcome these problems.

We hope you will take the time to provide us with some information about yourself, your organization, and your perceptions of male-female relationships in your professional life. How will this benefit you?

- Your experiences will contribute to a major sociological study.
- Answering the questions will stimulate your own thoughts on the subject.
- This process may encourage you to seek some new solutions to problems you've identified.
- We think you'll have fun, too!

The outcome will be a book written for men and women who are seeking ways to reach across gender differences to increase personal and organizational effectiveness.

We think you'll find this a rewarding experience, so read on, complete the questionnaire, and return it to us in the enclosed envelope no later than September 15. Thank you for your assistance in this important research.

Sincerely,

Lois B. Hart

Dr. Lois B. Hart

J. David Dalke

Dr. J. David Dalke

enc.

Part I

To help you focus on the questions, first identify, with initials, three women who fit the following relationships that you've had within the last two years.

Someone who was:

Your boss _____

Your peer/colleague _____

Your subordinate _____

However, if you have not had someone in each category, do not fret because we recognize that you may not have worked with women in each type of relationship.

Part II

The following twelve statements reflect problems that often exist in professional settings between men and women. Read each one and indicate if you have ever had a problem in that area, causing discomfort in your relationship. If you answer "YES," circle with whom you've experienced this problem—the boss, peer, or subordinate whom you identified in Part I. If you answer "NO," go on to the next category.

1. Have you ever had a problem with etiquette such as opening doors, shaking hands, or paying for meals/drinks?
   YES (1)   NO (2)
   a. With whom have you had this problem? (Circle all that apply)
   Boss (1)   Peer (2)   Subordinate (3)

2. Have you ever had a problem with language such as how you describe women (girl vs. woman vs. lady or with titles such as chairperson vs. chairman)?
   YES (1)   NO (2)
   a. With whom have you had this problem? (Circle all that apply)
   Boss (1)   Peer (2)   Subordinate (3)

3. Have you ever had a problem expressing your emotions with these individuals?
   YES (1)   NO (2)

a. With whom have you had this problem? (Circle all that apply)
Boss (1)   Peer (2)   Subordinate (3)

4. Have you ever exhibited inappropriate sexual behaviors/language such as sexy jokes, remarks about the woman's attractiveness or dress, made propositions?
YES (1)   NO (2)
a. With whom have you had this problem? (Circle all that apply)
Boss (1)   Peer (2)   Subordinate (3)

5. Have you ever been excessively distracted because of sexual attractiveness of these individuals?
YES (1)   NO (2)
a. With whom have you had this problem? (Circle all that apply)
Boss (1)   Peer (2)   Subordinate (3)

6. Have you ever had a problem in meetings accepting women's ideas, sharing power with them, or giving them recognition for their abilities and skills?
YES (1)   NO (2)
a. With whom have you had this problem? (Circle all that apply)
Boss (1)   Peer (2)   Subordinate (3)

7. Have you ever undermined the authority that comes with the woman's position?
YES (1)   NO (2)
a. With whom have you had this problem? (Circle all that apply)
Boss (1)   Peer (2)   Subordinate (3)

8. Have you ever questioned why women work?
YES (1)   NO (2)
a. With whom have you had this problem? (Circle all that apply)
Boss (1)   Peer (2)   Subordinate (3)

9. Have you ever established a different set of expectations for her job than what you might establish for a man?
YES (1)   NO (2)
a. With whom have you had this problem? (Circle all that apply)
Boss (1)   Peer (2)   Subordinate (3)

10. Have you ever had difficulty identifying or obtaining opportunities for her advancement?
YES (1)   NO (2)

a. With whom have you had this problem? (Circle all that apply.)
Boss (1)   Peer (2)   Subordinate (3)

11. Have you ever had the problem of determining how to keep her personal life separate from work and to what degree your organization should provide answers to practical problems such as child care and flexi-time?
YES (1)   NO (2)
a. With whom have you had this problem? (Circle all that apply)
Boss (1)   Peer (2)   Subordinate (3)

12. Have you been aware of the fact that the woman may not be receiving the same privileges, salary, or benefits as a man and/or been unable to resolve these discrepancies?
YES (1)   NO (2)
a. With whom have you had this problem? (Circle all that apply)
Boss (1)   Peer (2)   Subordinate (3)

Part III

Reflecting upon the problems you have had working with women, please indicate how much of a problem you've experienced overall in each problem area, with 1 being a minor problem and 5 being a major problem.

PROBLEM AREAS	Minor Problem				Major Problem	Not Applicable
Etiquette	1	2	3	4	5	6
Language	1	2	3	4	5	6
Emotions	1	2	3	4	5	6
Sexual Behaviors/ Language	1	2	3	4	5	6
Sexual Attractiveness	1	2	3	4	5	6
Meetings	1	2	3	4	5	6
Authority	1	2	3	4	5	6
Motivation to Work	1	2	3	4	5	6
Opportunities	1	2	3	4	5	6
Separating Work and Personal Life	1	2	3	4	5	6
Fewer Privileges/Benefits/ Money	1	2	3	4	5	6

Part IV

Although we are interested in comparing the problems encountered by women and men at work, we are mostly interested in how these problems are being faced and resolved. We need more details about the three problems with which you've had the most difficulty. In the appropriate spaces, fill in this information:

1. *Problem Area:*   Write the name of the problem area.

2. *Relationship:*   Check the relationship you'd like to write about, how long you've known her, and the difference in age between you.

3. *Example:*   Give an example of the kind of problem you've been having in this category.

4. *Resolution:*   Describe any and all attempts you've made to resolve this problem.

5. *Success:*   Mark the point on the scale that represents how successful you think you were in resolving this problem.

A.   Problem 1

     1. Problem area: _____

     2. Relationship (circle only one)
         a. Type

Boss	1
Peer	2
Subordinate	3

         b. Length

Less than 1 year	1
1-2 years	2
2 or more years	3

         c. Age difference (estimated)

Less than 10 years	1
10-19 years	2
20-29 years	3
30 years or more	4

     3. Example of problem:

4. Efforts made to resolve the problem:

	Low Degree				High Degree
5. Degree of success	1	2	3	4	5

B. Problem 2

1. Problem area: _____

2. Relationship (circle only one)
   a. Type
   Boss 1
   Peer 2
   Subordinate 3
   b. Length
   Less than 1 year 1
   1-2 years 2
   2 or more 3
   c. Age difference (estimated)
   Less than 10 years 1
   10-19 years 2
   20-29 years 3
   30 years or more 4

3. Example of problem:

4. Efforts made to resolve the problem:

	Low Degree				High Degree
5. Degree of success	1	2	3	4	5

C. Problem 3

   1. Problem area: _____

   2. Relationship (circle only one)
     a. Type
       Boss 1
       Peer 2
       Subordinate 3
     b. Length
       Less than 1 year 1
       1-2 years 2
       2 or more 3
     c. Age difference (estimated)
       Less than 10 years 1
       10-19 years 2
       20-29 years 3
       30 years or more 4

   3. Example of problem:

   4. Efforts made to resolve the problem:

	Low degree				High degree
5. Degree of success	1	2	3	4	5

Part V: About You

For statistical purposes only, we need to have the following demographic information:

   1. What type of business organization
      are you currently working in?
       Business/Industry 1
       Non-profit (Church Association, Health, Education) 2
       Government 3
   2. What is your level of management?
       Upper management 1
       Middle management 2

Supervisory level 3
Professional/Technical 4
Clerical 5
Other (specify) _____ 6

3. What state do you work in?

_____

4. Which age group are you in?
   Under 25 1
   25-34 2
   35-44 3
   45-54 4
   55 and over 5

5. Concerning your ethnic background, do you consider yourself to be:
   Anglo 1
   Black 2
   Hispanic 3
   Other (specify) _____ 4

6. What is your marital status?
   Married 1
   Unmarried 2

Part VI

For further data gathering: If we find it necessary, would you be willing to be interviewed as a follow-up on your information?

_____No _____Yes (please list below)

Name: _____

Address: _____

_____

Phone: _____ (list best time to call)

Would you name other persons who might answer a questionnaire?

Name: _____

Address: _____

_____

Name: _____

Address: _____

_____

Thank you for your time, energy, and information. Please return the completed questionnaire to Leadership Dynamics.

APPENDIX I:
WOMEN'S VERSION

Leadership ⋀ Dynamics

Dr. Lois B. Hart • (303) 823-5146   Box 320 • Lyons, Co. 80540

August 29, 198X

Dear Colleague:

We have selected you to participate in an important research study. We are trying to determine the extent of professional and personal conflict between men and women within the work environment, which we know exists based on our experience and current literature. Our main purpose is to identify strategies to overcome these problems.

We hope you will take the time to provide us with some information about yourself, your organization, and your perceptions of male-female relationships in your professional life. How will this benefit you?

- Your experiences will contribute to a major sociological study.
- Answering the questions will stimulate your own thoughts on the subject.
- This process may encourage you to seek some new solutions to problems you've identified.
- We think you'll have fun, too!

The outcome will be a book written for men and women who are seeking ways to reach across gender differences to increase personal and organizational effectiveness.

We think you'll find this a rewarding experience, so read on, complete the questionnaire, and return it to us in the enclosed envelope no later than September 15. Thank you for your assistance in this important research.

Sincerely,

Lois B. Hart

Dr. Lois B. Hart

J. David Dalke

Dr. J. David Dalke

enc.

Part I

To help you focus on the questions, first identify, with initials, three men who fit the following relationships that you've had within the last two years:

Someone who was:

Your boss _____

Your peer/colleague _____

Your subordinate _____

However, if you have not had someone in each category, do not fret because we recognize that you may not have worked with men in each type of relationship.

Part II

The following twelve statements reflect problems that often exist in professional settings between men and women. Read each one and indicate if you have ever had a problem in that area, causing discomfort in your relationship. If you answer "YES," circle with whom you've experienced this problem—the boss, peer, or subordinate whom you identified in Part I. If you answer "NO," go on to the next category.

1. Have you ever had a problem with etiquette such as opening doors, shaking hands, or paying for meals/drinks?
   YES (1)   NO (2)
   a. With whom have you had this problem? (Circle all that apply)
   Boss (1)   Peer (2)   Subordinate (3)

2. Have you ever had a problem with language such as how you describe yourself or other women (girl vs. woman vs. lady; or chairman vs. chairperson)?
   YES (1)   NO (2)
   a. With whom have you had this problem? (Circle all that apply)
   Boss (1)   Peer (2)   Subordinate (3)

3. Have you ever had a problem with your expression of emotions?
   YES (1)   NO (2)
   a. With whom have you had this problem? (Circle all that apply)
   Boss (1)   Peer (2)   Subordinate (3)

4. Have you ever had a problem as a recipient of inappropriate sexual behavior/language such as remarks, propositions?
   YES (1)   NO (2)
   a. With whom have you had this problem? (Circle all that apply)
   Boss (1)   Peer (2)   Subordinate (3)

5. Have you ever been excessively distracted because of sexual attractiveness of these individuals?
   YES (1)   NO (2)
   a. With whom have you had this problem? (Circle all that apply)
   Boss (1)   Peer (2)   Subordinate (3)

6. Have you ever had a problem in meetings convincing others of your ideas, to share power, or to receive recognition for your abilities and skills?
   YES (1)   NO (2)
   a. With whom have you had this problem? (Circle all that apply)
   Boss (1)   Peer (2)   Subordinate (3)

7. Have you ever had a problem convincing others to accept the authority that comes with your position?
   YES (1)   NO (2)
   a. With whom have you had this problem? (Circle all that apply)
   Boss (1)   Peer (2)   Subordinate (3)

8. Have you ever been questioned why you work?
   YES (1)   NO (2)
   a. With whom have you had this problem? (Circle all that apply)
   Boss (1)   Peer (2)   Subordinate (3)

9. Have you ever had a problem accepting or resolving a different set of expectations for your job than what a man might be given?
   YES (1)   NO (2)
   a. With whom have you had this problem? (Circle all that apply)
   Boss (1)   Peer (2)   Subordinate (3)

10. Have you ever had a problem obtaining opportunities for advancement from your boss?
    YES (1)   NO (2)
    a. With whom have you had this problem? (Circle all that apply)
    Boss (1)   Peer (2)   Subordinate (3)

11. Have you ever had the problem of separating your work from your home responsibilities or solving practical personal problems such as

child care, demands for overtime, or flexi-time?
YES (1)   NO (2)
a. With whom have you had this problem? (Circle all that apply)
Boss (1)   Peer (2)   Subordinate (3)

12. Have you ever had a problem resolving the fact that you may be receiving fewer privileges and benefits and lower salary than a man might?
YES (1)   NO (2)
a. With whom have you had this problem? (Circle all that apply)
Boss (1)   Peer (2)   Subordinate (3)

Part III
Reflecting upon the problems you have had working with men, please indicate how much of a problem you've experienced overall in each problem area, with 1 being a minor problem and 5 being a major problem.

PROBLEM AREAS	Minor Problem				Major Problem	Not Applicable
Etiquette	1	2	3	4	5	6
Language	1	2	3	4	5	6
Emotions	1	2	3	4	5	6
Sexual Behaviors/ Language	1	2	3	4	5	6
Sexual Attractiveness	1	2	3	4	5	6
Meetings	1	2	3	4	5	6
Authority	1	2	3	4	5	6
Motivation to Work	1	2	3	4	5	6
Opportunities	1	2	3	4	5	6
Separating Work and Personal Life	1	2	3	4	5	6
Fewer Privileges/ Benefits/Money	1	2	3	4	5	6

Part IV
Although we are interested in comparing the problems encountered by women and men at work, we are mostly interested in how these problems are being faced and resolved. We need more details about the three

problems with which you've had the most difficulty. In the appropriate spaces, fill in this information:

1. *Problem Area:*   Write the name of the problem area.
2. *Relationship:*   Check the relationship you'd like to write about, how long you've known him, and the difference in age between you.
3. *Example:*   Give an example of the kind of problem you've been having in this category.
4. *Resolution:*   Describe any and all attempts you've made to resolve this problem.
5. *Success:*   Mark the point on the scale that represents how successful you think you were in resolving this problem.

A.   Problem 1

    1. Problem area: _____

    2. Relationship (circle only one)
      a. Type
        Boss 1
        Peer 2
        Subordinate 3
      b. Length
        Less than 1 year 1
        1-2 years 2
        2 or more 3
      c. Age difference (estimated)
        Less than 10 years 1
        10-19 years 2
        20-29 years 3
        30 years or more 4

    3. Example of problem:

    4. Efforts made to resolve the problem:

                     Low degree   High degree
    5. Degree of success   1   2   3   4   5

B.   Problem 2

    1. Problem area: _____

    2. Relationship (circle only one)
      a. Type
         Boss 1
         Peer 2
         Subordinate 3
      b. Length
         Less than 1 year 1
         1-2 years 2
         2 or more 3
      c. Age difference (estimated)
         Less than 10 years 1
         10-19 years 2
         20-29 years 3
         30 years or more 4

    3. Examples of problem:

    4. Efforts made to resolve the problem:

                           Low degree   High degree
    5. Degree of success   1   2   3   4   5

C.   Problem 3

    1. Problem area: _____

    2. Relationship (circle only one)
      a. Type
         Boss 1
         Peer 2
         Subordinate 3

b. Length
   Less than 1 year 1
   1-2 years 2
   2 or more 3
c. Age difference (estimated)
   Less than 10 years 1
   10-19 years 2
   20-29 years 3
   30 years or more 4

3. Examples of problem:

4. Efforts made to resolve the problem:

	Low degree				High degree
5. Degree of success	1	2	3	4	5

Part V: About You
For statistical purposes only, we need to have the following demographic information:

1. What type of business organization
   are you currently working in?
   Business/Industry 1
   Non-profit (Church Association, Health, Education) 2
   Government 3
2. What is your level of management?
   Upper management 1
   Middle management 2
   Supervisory level 3
   Professional/Technical 4
   Clerical 5
   Other (specify)——————————. 6
3. What state do you work in?
   ——————————————

4. Which age group are you in?
   Under 25 1
   25-34 2
   35-44 3
   45-54 4
   55 and over 5
5. Concerning your ethnic background, do you consider yourself to be:
   Anglo 1
   Black 2
   Hispanic 3
   Other (specify) _____ 4
6. What is your marital status?
   Married 1
   Unmarried 2

Part VI
For further data gathering: If we find it necessary, would you be willing to be interviewed as a follow-up on your information?

_____No _____Yes (please list below)

Name: _____

Address: _____

_____

Phone: _____ (list best time to call)

Would you name other persons who might answer a questionnaire?

Name: _____

Address: _____

_____

Name: _____

Address: _____

_____

Thank you for your time, energy, and information. Please return the completed questionnaire to Leadership Dynamics.

APPENDIX II

The second major decision we made was who could give us the information we needed from among all working people. We used these criteria to select our sample:

1. *Professional.* Each person was in a professional role, either full- or part-time.
2. *Roles.* Each was or had been in a position of authority within the past two years.
3. *Type of Organization.* Our overall sample represented both profit and nonprofit organizations: business, industry, banks, education, medical associations, religious organizations, military, and government.
4. *Diversity.* Our overall sample represented diversity of age, race, and ethnic groups.
5. *Geography.* Those contacted lived in different parts of the United States and in Ontario, Canada.
6. *Attitude.* We talked and corresponded only with those who admitted that there were many problems between men and women and who were interested in finding solutions. We studied those who were on the "cutting edge" of change, those who thought deeply about these problems, and those who had caused or been hurt by the pain of societal adjustment, but who believed in the justice and possibility of change.

We initially distributed 500 questionnaires, primarily by mail, in August of 1981. Some were distributed personally in workshops and during speeches as described later in this appendix. Approximately 300 were given to women and 200 to men. Responses coming back to us totaled fifty-five from men and ninety-two from women, and their backgrounds fell into the categories listed in Table A-1.

TABLE A-1

	MEN	WOMEN
Level of Role in Organization		
Upper Management	20	17
Middle Management	16	30
Supervisory	1	12
Professional/Technical	9	22

TABLE A-1 (continued)

Level of Role in Organization	MEN	WOMEN
Clerical	0	2
Other (including volunteer, clinical consultants, sales)	4	4
Type of Organizations		
Business/Industry	23	25
Nonprofit (church, associations, health)	22	49
Government	5	13
Age		
Under 25	0	0
26-34	12	28
35-44	26	44
45-54	11	13
55 and over	1	2
Ethnicity/Race		
Anglo	49	81
Black	1	3
Hispanic	0	3
Marital Status		
Married	38	53
Unmarried	12	34

TABLE A-2 Geographic Locations of Both Men and Women Respondents[a]

California	5	Minnesota	1
Colorado	55	North Carolina	2
Connecticut	1	New York	6
District of Columbia	7	Ohio	2
Florida	2	Oregon	1
Illinois	1	Rhode Island	1
Indiana	1	Texas	1
Kansas	24	Utah	1
Massachusetts	4	Wyoming	1
Michigan	19	Ontario, Canada	2

[a]Demographic Data Was Omitted on Five Respondents' Questionnaires.

We used four additional methods to gather the information we needed. First, as we reviewed the written data, we contacted individuals for further elaboration of a problem described on the questionnaire. Some interviews were quite lengthy. Details about these interviews are found within the text, along with the key ideas they gave us.

Second, we used the questionnaire in workshops held throughout the year of our research, giving a total of 500 additional people contacted in order to validate the patterns we observed in the written data.

Third, we talked about our research informally in both professional and personal settings, supplementing our other methods.

Fourth, we held two formal research "focus groups" with 50 selected men and women in Colorado. The first, held in the fall of 1980, helped us to delineate the problems. The second, held in the spring of 1981, was a collaborative effort to identify additional solutions to the problems we had been studying.

INDEX